To Live From The Heart

MINDFUL PATHS TO THE SACRED

www.transworldbooks.co.uk
www.transworldireland.ie

To Live From The Heart

MINDFUL PATHS TO THE SACRED

Edited by Sister Stan

TRANSWORLD IRELAND

TRANSWORLD IRELAND PUBLISHERS
28 Lower Leeson Street, Dublin 2, Ireland
www.transworldireland.ie

Transworld Ireland is part of the Penguin Random House group of companies
whose addresses can be found at global.penguinrandomhouse.com

First published in the UK and Ireland in 2015
by Transworld Ireland
an imprint of Transworld Publishers

Every effort has been made to obtain the necessary permissions with
reference to copyright material, both illustrative and quoted. We apologize
for any omissions in this respect and will be pleased to make the appropriate
acknowledgements in any future edition.

A CIP catalogue record for this book is available from the British Library.

ISBN 9781848272279

Typeset in 10½/15pt Berkeley Oldstyle by Kestrel Data, Exeter, Devon.
Printed and bound by Clays Ltd, Bungay, Suffolk.

Penguin Random House is committed to a sustainable future
for our business, our readers and our planet. This book is made
from Forest Stewardship Council® certified paper.

1 3 5 7 9 10 8 6 4 2

This book is dedicated to all of
those seeking truth.
Prayer is raising and opening
the mind and heart to God,
with or without words.

Acknowledgements

With profound gratefulness and thanks to Brenda Kimber of Transworld for her support, interest and dedication, to Johanne Farrelly for typing various versions of the book, to the contributors, Sr Aneta, Sr Marie Fahy, Br Richard Hendrick OFM Cap, Sr Mary Magdalen, Anne Marie Maguire, Sr Regina McHugh, Sr Bernadine Meskell, John O'Donohue and Jean Vanier for their inspiring essays and to the countless people who have made it possible to conceive to write and to produce this book and to put it into your hands, and to you the reader for your interest.

Contents

Dedication   v
Acknowledgements   vii

Introduction   xiii

In Wonder   1
They Receive Each Day As An Invitation –   23
John O'Donohue

In Gratitude   49
Growing in Prayer – A member of the Poor Clare   60
Sisters

In Surrender   87
Prayer – Sr Mary Magdalen, Carmelite Sister   93

In Trust   113
Prayer is the Most Human and Personal Thing   127
We Do – Sr Bernardine Meskell, Poor Clare Sister

In Praise   133

In Love   151
Letter to Sister Stan – Sr Marie Fahy,   156
Cistercian Sister

For Serenity   193
The Contemplative Life – Anne Marie Maguire   212

For Protection   225

For Faith   243
What does prayer mean to me? – Sr Regina McHugh,   245
Poor Clare Sisters

Celtic Christianity – Brother Richard Hendrick   266
OFM Cap

For Peace   281
Contemplative Prayer – Sr Aneta, Redemptoristin   285

For Blessings   301
To Pray is to Love – Jean Vanier   305

Contributors' Biographies   318

Dear God help me to spread your beauty
everywhere I go today.
Flood my soul with your Spirit and light.
Fill my whole being so utterly that all my life may
only be a radiance of you.
Shine through me and be so much a part of me,
That every soul I meet may see your presence in me.
Let them look at me and find no longer me but you.
Stay with me and then I will begin to shine
as you shine
So to be a light for others.
Let me preach you without preaching;
Teach you without teaching, not by words
but by example;
By the catching influence of who I am and what I do;
And by the obvious fullness of the love my heart
holds for you.

Cardinal Newman

Introduction

This is a sacred treasury, a spiritual notebook which is special to me, and which has touched and inspired me at different times over the years.

All of these prayers have come to me from many different people, traditions, cultures, faiths and religions. They came to me through different versions of the Bible and prayer books, as well as other books and individuals. Some are well known, others less so.

Prayer is opening up the mind and heart to God. Over the years at different times these prayers have opened my heart and mind and my whole being to my God and given expression to my heart's yearning for his presence.

Meister Eckhart tells us, 'the nearest thing to God

is silence'. These prayers have led me into the silence and the stillness of my innermost being. As you read or dip into this book I encourage you to stay with it and allow it to move you into that place of quiet stillness where you can be fully present with yourself and your God.

I am sharing these prayers with you because I believe they have the capacity to move you as they moved me.

I hope too they may inspire you to make your own sacred treasury and to share them with others.

Meister Eckhart said if the only prayer you ever said was thank you, it is enough. If this little book fills you with gratitude, it is enough.

Sister Stan, 2015

In Wonder

To see a World in a Grain of Sand,
    And a Heaven in a Wild Flower,
Hold Infinity in the palm of your hand,
    And Eternity in an hour.

William Blake

*I believe a leaf of grass is no less than
the journey-work of the stars*

WALT WHITMAN

*What lies behind us and what lies
before us are tiny matters compared
to what lies within us*

RALPH WALDO EMERSON

Every blade of grass has its angel that bends over it
And whispers, 'Grow, grow'

The Talmud

Earth's crammed with heaven,
And every common bush afire with God;
But only he who sees, takes off his shoes,
The rest sit round it and pluck blackberries

Elizabeth Barrett Browning

A man should hear a little music, read a little poetry, and see a fine picture every day of his life, in order that worldly cares may not obliterate the sense of the beautiful which God has implanted in the human soul.

JOHANN WOLFGANG VON GOETHE

The world stands out on either side
No wider than the heart is wide;
Above the world is stretched the sky,
No higher than the soul is high.

Edna St Vincent Millay

Each of us needs to withdraw from the cares which will not withdraw from us. We need hours of aimless wandering, or spates of time sitting on park benches, observing the mysterious world of ants and the canopy of tree tops. May each of us have this opportunity in our life.

MAYA ANGELOU, from *WOULDN'T TAKE NOTHING FOR MY JOURNEY NOW*

Our deepest fear is not that we are inadequate. Our deepest fear is that we are powerful beyond measure. It is our light, not our darkness that most frightens us. We were born to make manifest the glory of God that is within us. It is not just in some of us; it is in everyone and as we let our own light shine, we unconsciously give others permission to do the same. As we are liberated from our own fear, our presence automatically liberates others.

MARIANNE WILLIAMSON

*I did not know that the sun, the moon,
the evening star, were the words with which he
spoke to me, so I never heard their song,
their cry, their cosmic silence.*

TONY DE MELLO

*We can be sure that, if we consider every
choice carefully, and seek divine guidance,
our decisions will please God.*

ST MORGAN

Longing

O God, you are my God, for you I long,
for you my soul is thirsting.
My body pines for you
like a dry, weary land without water.
So I gaze on you in the sanctuary
to see your strength and your glory.

For your love is better than life,
my lips will speak your praise.
So I will bless you all my life,
in your name I will lift up my hands.
My soul shall be filled as with a banquet,
my mouth shall praise you with joy.

On my bed I remember you.
On you I muse through the night.
For you have been my help;
in the shadow of your wings I rejoice.
My soul clings to you;
your right hand holds me fast

Psalm 62/63: 2–9

In the beginning was the Word, and the Word was with God, and the Word was God. He was with God in the beginning. Through him all things came to be; not one thing had its being but through him. All that came to be had life in him and that life was the light of men. A light that shines in the dark, a light that darkness could not overpower.

John 1: 1–5

*In truth no one is totally evil or totally good;
every person at every moment is capable of
choosing good or choosing evil.*

St Morgan

*I am one of the countless particles of dust that
dance in the rays of the universal sun.*

Tony de Mello

Yahweh you examine me and know me
You know if I am standing or sitting
You read my thoughts from afar
Whether I walk or lie down, you are watching
You know every detail of my conduct.

The word is not even on my tongue
Yahweh, before you know all about it;
Close behind me and close in front
You fence me round
shielding me with your hand
Such knowledge is beyond my understanding,
a height to which my mind cannot attain

Where could I go to escape your spirit?
Where could I flee from your presence?
If I climb to the heavens, you are there,
there too if I lie in the depths

(*Continued*)

If I flew to the point of sunrise
or westward across the sea
your hand would still be guiding me
your right hand holding me

If I asked darkness to cover me
and light to become night around me
that darkness would not be dark to you
night would be as light as day

Psalm 139: 1–12

Those who contemplate the beauty of the earth find reserves of strength that will endure as long as life lasts. There is something infinitely healing in the repeated refrains of nature – the assurance that dawn comes after night, and spring after winter.

RACHEL CARSON, *SILENT SPRING*

What would the world be, once bereft
Of wet and of wildness? Let them be left,
O let them be left, wildness and wet;
Long live the weeds and the wilderness yet.

Gerard Manley Hopkins, 'Inversnaid'

*It is a wholesome and necessary thing for
us to turn again to the earth and in the
contemplation of her beauties to know of the
sense of wonder and humility*

RACHEL CARSON, *THE SENSE OF WONDER*

Last night as I was sleeping.
I dreamt – marvelous error! –
that I had a beehive
here inside my heart. And the golden bees
were making white combs
and sweet honey
from my old failures.

Antonio Machado

The world is charged with the grandeur of God.
It will flame out, like shining from shook foil;
It gathers to a greatness, like the ooze of oil
Crushed. Why do men then now not reck his rod?
Generations have trod, have trod, have trod;
And all is seared with trade; bleared, smeared with toil;
And wears man's smudge and shares
man's smell: the soil
Is bare now, nor can foot feel, being shod.

And for all this, nature is never spent;
There lives the dearest freshness deep down things;
And though the last lights off the black West went
Oh, morning, at the brown brink eastward, springs—
Because the Holy Ghost over the bent
World broods with warm breast and
with ah! bright wings.

Gerard Manley Hopkins, 'God's Grandeur'

In the beginning was God,
Today is God,
Tomorrow will be God.
Who can make an image of God?
He has no body.
He is the word which comes out of your mouth.
That word!
It is no more,
It is past, and still it lives!
So is God.

A Pygmy prayer

We can make our minds so like still water that beings gather about us that they may see, it may be, their own images, and so live for a moment with a clearer, perhaps even with a fiercer life because of our quiet.

WILLIAM BUTLER YEATS, *THE CELTIC TWILIGHT*

All this hurrying soon will be over
Only when we tarry do we touch the holy

Rainer Marie Rilke

God of the Universe
You speak to us in all creation
But you call us most surely in the depths of our hearts
Help us to listen to your voice today
Gentling our work, our recreation
and our relationships with others
in ways that let us hear you

Sr Stan

They Receive Each Day As An Invitation

John O'Donohue

One night recently, I visited our family farm. A calf had just been born. It had just slumped to earth in a wet, steaming mass. At midnight, I went out to look at the cow again; by this time she had licked her new calf dry and he had sucked his first milk. Everything was mild and gentle, illuminated by the moon's mint light. What a beautiful night it was to arrive on earth. Even if this newborn were a genius, it could never possibly imagine the surprise of the world that was waiting when the dawn would break in a miracle of colour illuminating the personality of mountains, river and sky.

The liturgy of dawn signals the wonder of the arriving day. The magic of darkness breaking through into colour and light is such a promise of invitation and possibility. No wonder we always associate hope and urgency of new beginning with the dawn. Each day is the field of brightness where the invitation of our life unfolds. A new day is an intricate and subtle matrix; written into its mystery are the happenings sent to awaken and challenge us.

No day is ever the same, and no day stands still; each one moves through a different territory, awakening new beginnings. A day moves forward in moments and once a moment has flickered into life, it vanishes and is replaced by the next. It is fascinating that this is where we live, within an emerging lacework that continuously unravels. Often a fleeting moment can hold a whole sequence of the future in distilled form: that unprepared second when you looked in a parent's eye and saw death already beginning to loom. Or the second you noticed a softening in someone's voice and you knew that a friendship was beginning. Or catching your partner's gaze upon you and knowing the love that surrounded you. Each day is seeded with recognitions.

The writing life is a wonderful metaphor for this. The writer goes to his desk each morning to meet the empty white page. As he settles himself, he is preparing for visitation and voyage. His memory, longing and craft set the frame for what might emerge. He has no idea what will come. Yet despite his limitations, his creative work will find its own direction to form. Each of us is an artist of our days; the greater our integrity and awareness, the more original and creative our time will become.

(from *Benedictus* by John O'Donohue)

The light of God surrounds me
The love of God enfolds me
The power of God protects me
The presence of God watches over me
Wherever I am, God is

James Dillet Freeman

Behold the lilies of the field
They neither sew nor spin
Yet not even Solomon
In all his glory
Was clothed like one of these

Luke 12: 27

Angel nor Saint have I seen
But I heard the roar of the western sea
And the isle of my heart is in the midst of it

St Columba

I weave into my life this day
the presence of God upon my way.
I weave into the darkest night
Strands of God all shining bright.
I weave into each deed that's done
Joy and hope of the risen Son

An Irish prayer

I wandered lonely as a cloud
That floats on high o'er vales and hills,
When all at once I saw a crowd,
A host, of golden daffodils;
Beside the lake, beneath the trees,
Fluttering and dancing in the breeze.

Continuous as the stars that shine
And twinkle on the Milky Way,
They stretched in never-ending line
Along the margin of a bay:
Ten thousand saw I at a glance,
Tossing their heads in sprightly dance.

The waves beside them danced, but they
Out-did the sparkling waves in glee:
A poet could not but be gay,
In such a jocund company:
I gazed – and gazed – but little thought
What wealth the show to me had brought:

For oft, when on my couch I lie
In vacant or in pensive mood,
They flash upon that inward eye
Which is the bliss of solitude;
And then my heart with pleasure fills,
And dances with the daffodils.

William Wordsworth, 'Daffodils'

Love is fed by the imagination, by which we become wiser than we know, better than we feel, nobler than we are: by which we can see life as a whole, by which and by which alone we can understand others in their real and their ideal relation.

OSCAR WILDE, *DE PROFUNDIS*

*Why do we rush about to the top of heaven
and the bottom of the earth looking for God,
who is here at home with us, if only we
would be at home with him?*

St Augustine

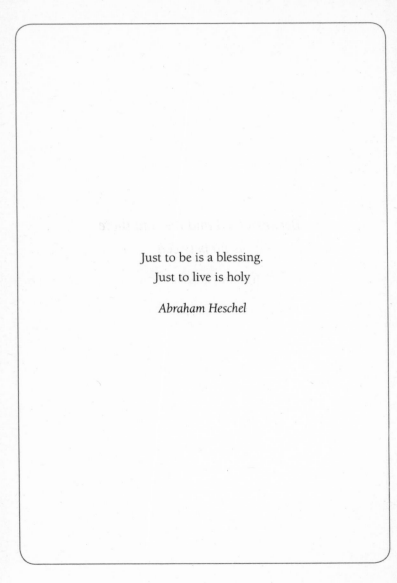

Just to be is a blessing.
Just to live is holy

Abraham Heschel

*Between God and the soul there
is no between*

Julian of Norwich

33

I arise today, through
The strength of heaven,
The light of the sun,
The radiance of the moon,
The splendour of fire,
The speed of lightning,
The swiftness of wind,
The depth of the sea,
The stability of the earth,
The firmness of rock.
I arise today, through
God's strength to pilot me,
God's might to uphold me,
God's wisdom to guide me,
God's eye to look before me,
God's ear to hear me,
God's word to speak for me,
God's hand to guard me,
God's shield to protect me,
God's host to save me
Christ with me,

Christ before me,
Christ behind me,
Christ in me,
Christ beneath me,
Christ above me,
Christ on my right,
Christ on my left,
Christ when I lie down,
Christ when I sit down,
Christ when I arise,
Christ in the heart of every man who thinks of me,
Christ in the mouth of everyone who speaks of me,
Christ in every eye that sees me,
Christ in every ear that hears me.
I arise today.

St Patrick's Breastplate

There exists only the present instant . . . a Now which always and without end is itself new. There is no yesterday nor any tomorrow, but only Now, as it was a thousand years ago and as it will be a thousand years hence

MEISTER ECKHART

The ground we walk on, the plants and creatures, the clouds above constantly dissolving into new formations – each gift of nature possessing its own radiant energy, bound together by cosmic harmony

RUTH BERNHARD

Sit quietly, do nothing
Spring comes and the grass grows by itself

Zen saying

Live in the present
Do the things you know need to be done.
Do all the good you can each day.
The future will unfold.

Peace Pilgrim

Behold the plant!
It is a butterfly
Fettered by the earth

Behold the butterfly!
It is a plant
Freed by the cosmos!

Rudolf Steiner

If you can keep your head when all about you
Are losing theirs and blaming it on you,
If you can trust yourself when all men doubt you,
But make allowance for their doubting too . . .

Rudyard Kipling

There is really nothing you must be and there is nothing you must do. There is really nothing you must have and there is nothing you must know. There is really nothing you must become. However, it helps to understand that fire burns, and when it rains, the earth gets wet

ZEN SAYING

The way you see people
Is the way you treat them
And the way you treat them
Is what they become

Johann Wolfgang von Goethe

The great deeds of mankind
are not those that make a lot of noise
Great things happen simply
Like the trickling of water
The flowing of air
And the growing of grain

Adalbert Stifter

Let us not look back in anger or forward in fear
But around us in awareness

James Thurber

Realise that, just as a bird
Needs two wings to fly,
Wisdom and compassion need
To be developed simultaneously

Matthieu Ricard

I am Not I

I am not I.
I am this one
walking beside me whom I do not see,
whom at times I manage to visit,
and whom at other times I forget;
who remains calm and silent while I talk,
and forgives, gently, when I hate,
who walks where I am not,
who will remain standing when I die.

Juan Ramón Jiménez, translated by Robert Bly

It is always springtime in the heart that loves God

St John Vianney

Love after Love

The time will come
when, with elation
you will greet yourself arriving
at your own door, in your own mirror
and each will smile at the other's welcome,

and say, sit here. Eat.
You will love again the stranger who was your self.
Give wine. Give bread. Give back your heart
to itself, to the stranger who has loved you

all your life, whom you ignored
for another, who knows you by heart.
Take down the love letters from the bookshelf,

the photographs, the desperate notes,
peel your own image from the mirror.
Sit. Feast on your life.

Derek Walcott

Do not stand at my grave and weep.
I am not there. I do not sleep.
I am a thousand winds that blow.
I am the diamond glints on snow.
I am the sunlight on ripened grain.
I am the gentle autumn rain.
When you awaken in the morning's hush
I am the swift uplifting rush
Of quiet birds in circled flight.
I am the soft stars that shine at night.
Do not stand at my grave and cry;
I am not there. I did not die.

Mary Elizabeth Frye

There is no shortage of good days.
It is good lives that are hard to come by.

Annie Dillard, The Writing Life

I believe in the sun
Even when it is not shining
I believe in love
Even when I can't feel it
I believe in God
Even when he is silent

A Jewish prayer

God in All Things

Apprehend God in all things,
for God is in all things.
Every single creature is full of God
and is a book about God.
Every creature is a word of God.
If I spent enough time with the tiniest creature –
even a caterpillar –
I would never have to prepare a sermon.
So full of God
is every creature.

Meister Eckhart

For Equilibrium:
A Blessing

Like the joy of the sea coming home to shore
May the relief of laughter rinse through your soul

John O'Donohue

As big soft buffetings come at the car sideways.
And catch the heart off guard and blow it open

Seamus Heaney, 'Postscript', in The Spirit Level

Sheep and Lambs

All in the April evening
April airs were abroad;
The sheep with their little lambs
Passed me by on the road.

The sheep with their little lambs
Passed me by on the road;
All in the April evening
I thought on the Lamb of God.

The lambs were weary and crying
With a weak, human cry.

I thought on the Lamb of God
Going meekly to die.

(*Continued*)

Up in the blue, blue mountains
Dewy pastures are sweet;
Rest for the little bodies,
Rest for the little feet.

But for the Lamb of God,
Up on the hill-top green,
Only a Cross of shame
Two stark crosses between.

All in the April evening,
April airs were abroad;
I saw the sheep with their lambs,
And thought on the Lamb of God.

Katharine Tynan

In Gratitude

He who knows that enough is enough
will always have enough

Lao Tzu

If the only prayer you say in your entire life
is 'thank you' that would suffice

Meister Eckhart

And forget not that the earth delights
to feel your bare feet
And the winds long to play
With your hair.

Kahlil Gibran

Be joyful, brothers and sisters. Keep your faith
and do the little things.

St David

Cultivate and share the fruits of the earth.

St Ailbe

*As we express our gratitude, we must never
forget that the highest appreciation is not to
utter words, but to live by them.*

John F. Kennedy

Look to this day:
For it is life, the very life of life.
In its brief course
Lie all the verities and realities of your existence.
The bliss of growth,
The glory of action,
The splendour of achievement
Are but experiences of time.
For yesterday is but a dream
And tomorrow is only a vision;
And today well-lived, makes
Yesterday a dream of happiness
And every tomorrow a vision of hope
Look well therefore to this day
Such is the salutation to the dawn.

Sanskrit Salutation to the Dawn

See in each herb and small animal, every bird and beast, and in each man and woman, the eternal Word of God.

St Ninian

You pray in your distress and in your need;
would that you might pray
also in the fullness of your joy
and in your days of abundance.

Kahlil Gibran

This food is the gift of the whole universe:
The earth, the sky and much hard work
May we live in a way that is worthy of this food
May we transform our unskilled states of mind
Especially that of greed
May we eat only foods that nourish and prevent illness
May we accept this food for the realisation
of the way of understanding and love

Thich Nhat Hanh

This is what you shall do: Love the earth and sun and the animals, despise riches, give alms to every one that asks, stand up for the stupid and crazy, devote your income and labor to others, hate tyrants, argue not concerning God, have patience and indulgence toward the people, take off your hat to nothing known or unknown or to any man or number of men, go freely with powerful uneducated persons and with the young and with the mothers of families, read these leaves in the open air every season of every year of your life, re-examine all you have been told at school or church or in any book, dismiss whatever insults your own soul, and your very flesh shall be a great poem and have the richest fluency not only in its words but in the silent lines of its lips and face and between the lashes of your eyes and in every motion and joint of your body.

Walt Whitman, Preface to Leaves of Grass

Night is drawing nigh
For all that has been:
Thanks.
For all that will be;
Yes.

Dag Hammarskjöld

Lord, if I hold your hand in the darkness,
It is enough
Since I know that although I stumble as I go,
You do not fall

An old Irish prayer

Rune of Hospitality

I saw a stranger yesterday,
I put food in the eating place,
Drink in the drinking place,
Music in the listening place;

And in the blessed name of the Trivine
He blessed myself and my house,
My cattle and my dear ones.

And the lark said in her song
It is often, often, often,
Goes the Christ in the stranger's guise
Often, often, often
Goes the Christ in the stranger's guise

An old Gaelic rune

Three things that please God are true faith in God with a pure heart, a simple life with a grateful spirit, and generosity inspired by charity. The three things that most displease God are a mouth that hates people, a heart harbouring resentments, and confidence in wealth.

St Ita

Growing in Prayer

A member of the
Poor Clare Sisters, Dublin

In every human heart, there is hunger for the Infinite, for some One – the One we come to know through the gift of faith. 'Jesus Christ is the beginning and the end, the alpha and omega, Lord of the universe, the great hidden key to human history.'[1]

We, the followers of St Clare, are a community of sisters wholly dedicated to prayer. The centre and highlight of our life is the daily Eucharist and we strive to give the Lord the praise that is due (Psalm 146: 1) seven times a day through the *Liturgy of the Hours*, the Prayer of the Church. We also spend an

---

1 From a homily by Pope Paul VI preached on 29 November 1970 in Manila, the Philippines, *Liturgy of the Hours* (Talbot Press, 1974), Vol. 3, 13th Sunday in Ordinary Time.

hour and a half (though not continuously) each day in private prayer with him.

Our prayer is our mission in the Church and the world. It touches every person. 'For me prayer is a surge of the heart: it is a simple look turned towards Heaven, it is a cry of recognition and of love, embracing both trial and joy.'[2] At prayer, we are blessed with exposition of the Blessed Sacrament in our little choir. In the silent hours of the night, and again throughout the day, our Eucharistic King is worshipped, loved and entreated. No one in the wide world is forgotten. Each and all are brought to the Heart of Infinite Mercy.

There are as many ways of praying as there are people. Nobody ever taught us how to relate to our parents, but because we loved them, and knew that they loved us, we communicated naturally, as need or the emotion of the moment dictated. We can always feel even more free to relate to our Heavenly Father and our Blessed Mother.

(Continued)

2 St Thérèse of Lisieux, *Manuscrits autobiographiques*, C 25r. CCC para. 2558.

Praying with Scripture

Lord, teach us to pray. (Luke. 11: 1)

Let us ask the Holy Spirit to teach us to pray and to help us hear him; to understand what he is asking of us; and for the grace to do what he is asking of us.

Thus says the Lord: 'I will lure her and will lead her out into the desert, and speak to her heart' (Hos. 2: 14). Our Poor Clare monastery is our monastic desert where we listen to and speak to Jesus: The Church wishes all her children to learn the surpassing knowledge of Jesus Christ by frequent reading of the divine Scriptures. However, prayer should accompany the reading of Sacred Scripture so that a dialogue takes place between God and man. For 'we speak to him when we pray; we listen to him when we read the divine word.'

Could there be a greater privilege in this life than to take part in a dialogue with God, whom we will see and enjoy for all eternity in heaven?

Through the Bible we meet the person of Jesus Christ. We come to learn who he is, how he lived, what he taught, what he has done for us, and it is through Scripture that we learn his plan of salvation and happiness for our lives. Reflecting on this truth, St Jerome said, 'Ignorance of Scripture is ignorance of Christ.'[3]

Our present Holy Father urges 'all Christians to renew their personal encounter with Jesus Christ, or at least to make the decision to let ourselves be found by Him, to seek Him every day without fail.'[4] This is an invitation to contemplative prayer.

Prayer of loving adoration

As Poor Clares, the prayer of loving adoration is our priority. Our Father, St Francis, knew this well. When he came into the presence of the Blessed Sacrament he really believed that our dear Lord was truly present. God was present, Body and Blood, Soul and Divinity, so he fell down in adoration. In the presence of the Blessed Sacrament we believe, and, as a consequence, we must adore. Where that impulse is missing it is because faith has weakened or perhaps

(Continued)

3 St Jerome, Catholic Biblical Commentary.
4 'Rejoice . . .', Letter to Religious, towards the special Year for the Consecrated Life.

is near death. This shows in other areas: as lack of faith in Christ's Vicar, in the Church's magisterium (teaching authority). This is always partnered with lack of adoration – the overspill of our love for God. The consequence of adoration must be exercised. We prostrate ourselves before God in body and spirit, and in heart.

Obstacles

There is much to reflect on about loving in complete surrender. It is not real surrender in our spiritual life unless it is complete, unless it is the work of love. Let us never be partially occupied with what we set out to do, but totally occupied like our Mother, St Clare and, indeed, all the saints. In this, we find rest and fulfilment: 'You may totally love Him, Who gave Himself totally for your love.'[5]

A great source of strength for St Clare was the totality with which she gave herself to her vocation. So she got up and she went, leaving everything behind. She was not concerned about the settlement of her

5 3rd letter of St Clare to St Agnes of Prague, quoted in *Francis and Clare: The Complete Works*, trans. R. J. Armstrong and I. C. Brady, 6th edition (New York: Paulist Press, 1982), p. 58.

estate; she was just single-minded! And when she left, she wore her best dress. Surely she should have brought warm, durable clothing for the kind of life she was going to live! But she went to the Portiuncula, that little chapel near Assisi, as if to a ball: she wore her best dress for Christ, to give it away – a perfect symbol of all she was leaving behind. She must have had footgear very unsuitable for that walk, too. Let us linger on these details, and enjoy thinking of them.

Clare was equally focused when it came to her family. She loved them more than any other earthly tie – but left them and, in the very leaving, found them on a much deeper level, the profound level of the heart of Christ. And consider the totality of her vision! Let us think for a moment of how much she asked of her daughters, of the things that shine out in her beautiful, simple Rule. Christ is my riches in poverty. There is a sweeping, free completeness. When we do not give ourselves totally, there is always a weight on the heart. Even the smallest self-concern is too heavy for one who is called to run as lightly as we are. Through the rocks of life, over the crags of temptation,

(Continued)

we are spiritually bare-footed. One has to be totally committed to do this. Why, after putting off all concerns, should we put them on again? Let us trust, not in ourselves, not in the circumstances we should like to alter or modify, but in God!

Conclusion

When God says to us each day, in one way or another, 'Come! Walk on the water', we must come, not putting our trust in the weather forecast. Our trust is in his word. Because he says 'Come', we come.

This 'Come' will be heard today if we listen. Let us not be 'things' persons, but 'values' persons, as St Clare was. We can do this by making the remote ideal proximate, the ultimate value immediate. This makes us rejoice. If God is present in the difficulties that arise, we can't brood, though we can certainly suffer. A great ideal inspires us to be 'values persons' – strong in making the ultimate immediate, full of trust because the remote is present, and totally given, so that, with St Clare's help, we may achieve the joy, lightness of heart and unwaveringness that characterize the beautiful woman we call St Clare.

Bibliography

Liturgy of the Hours, Vol. 3, 13th Sunday in Ordinary Time. Talbot Press, 1974

St Thérèse of Lisieux, *Manuscrits autobiographiques*

Catechism of the Catholic Church, 2nd edition, 1994

St Jerome, Catholic Biblical Commentary

'Rejoice . . .' Letter to Religious, towards the special Year for the Consecrated Life

3rd letter of St Clare to St Agnes of Prague: see *Francis and Clare: The Complete Works*, trans. R. J. Armstrong and I. C. Brady, 6th edition (New York: Paulist Press, 1982), p. 58

Enough

Great troubles come
From not knowing what is enough
Great conflict arises
From wanting too much
When we know when enough is enough
There will always be enough

Lao Tzu

In the wilderness you saw how the LORD your God carried you, just as one carries a child, all along the way you travelled until you reached this place, where you are now.

DEUTERONOMY 1: 31

No longer forward nor behind
I look in hope or fear;
But, grateful, take the good I find,
The best of now and here

John Greenleaf Whittier

For each new morning with its light,
For rest and shelter in the night,
For health and food, for love and friends,
For everything Thy goodness sends

Ralph Waldo Emerson

Be grateful for whatever comes
Because each has been sent
As a guide from beyond

Rumi

Web of butterflies
You butterfly creation!
You radiate
Something better than sunlight
You radiate
Spiral light
Into the cosmos

Rudolf Steiner

God's admiration for us is infinitely greater than anything we can conjure up for him

St Francis of Assisi

We thank Thee, Lord, for happy hearts,
For rain and sunny weather.
We thank Thee, Lord, for this our food,
And that we are together.

Unknown

I know of nothing else but Miracles . . .
To me, every hour of the light and dark is a miracle,
Every cubic inch of space is a miracle,
Every square yard of the surface of the earth
is spread with the same,
Every foot of the interior swarms with the same;
Every spear of grass – the frames, limbs, organs, of men
and women, and all that concerns them,
All these to me are unspeakably perfect miracles

Walt Whitman, Leaves of Grass

*The food which we are about to eat is
earth, water and sun,
Compounded through the alchemy of
many plants.
Therefore earth, water and sun will
become part of us.
This food is also the fruit of the labour
of many beings and creatures.
We are grateful for it.
Let it give us strength and joy and may it
increase our love.*

A UNITARIAN PRAYER

*Be very constant in your prayers for the
faithful departed, as if each dead person
were a personal friend of yours.*

St Columba (Columcille)

*The bread is pure and fresh
The water is cool and clear
Lord of all life be with us
Lord of all life be near*

African grace

One looks back with appreciation to the brilliant teachers, but with gratitude to those who touched our human feelings. The curriculum is so much necessary raw material, but warmth is the vital element for the growing plant and for the soul of the child.

CARL JUNG

Be with me, O God, at breaking of bread,
Be with me, O God, at the close of my meal;
Let no whit adown my body,
That may hurt my sorrowing soul.
O no whit adown my body,
that may hurt my sorrowing soul.

Gaelic grace

This ritual is One.
The food is One.
We who offer the food are One.
The fire of hunger is also One.
All action is One.
We who understand this are One.

Traditional Hindu blessing

Gratitude unlocks the fullness of life. It turns what we have into enough, and more. It turns denial into acceptance, chaos to order, confusion to clarity. It can turn a meal into a feast, a house into a home, a stranger into a friend.

MELODY BEATTIE

The journey is the reward

TAO SAYING

It was you who created my inmost being
And put me together in my mother's womb
For all the mysteries I thank you
For the wonder of myself for the wonder of your works
You know me through and through
From having watched my bones take shape
When I had been joined in secret
Knitted together in the limbo of the womb
You had scrutinized my every action
All were recorded in your book;
My days listed and determined,
even before the first of them occurred
God, how hard it is to grasp your thoughts
How impossible to count them!
I could no more count them than I could the sand
and suppose I could, you would still be with me.

Psalm 138/139: 12–18

Give thanks to the Lord for he is good
For his love endures forever.
Let the sons of Israel say
His love endures forever.
Let the sons of Aaron say
His love endures forever.
Let those who fear the Lord say
His love endures forever.
I called to the Lord in my distress
He answered and freed me.
The Lord is at my side, I do not fear
What can man do against me.
The Lord is at my side as my helper
I shall look down on my foes.
It is better to take refuge in the Lord
Than to trust in men.
It is better to take refuge with the Lord
Than to trust in princes.

Psalm 117: 1–9

Lord, behold our family here assembled. We thank Thee for this place in which we dwell; for the love that unites us; for the peace accorded us this day; for the hope with which we expect the morrow; for the health, the work, the food, and the bright skies that make our lives delightful; for our friends in all parts of the earth . . . Amen

ROBERT LOUIS STEVENSON

Lord, I am grateful to you
That in your mysterious love
You have taken away from me
All earthly wealth,
And that you now clothe and feed me
Through the kindness of others.

Lord, I am grateful to you
For since you have taken away from me
the sight of my eyes
You care for me now
through the eyes of others.

Lord, I am grateful to you
That since you have taken away from me
the strength of my hands and heart
You care for me now
through the hands and hearts of others.

Lord, I pray for them,
That you will reward them in your love
That they may continue to faithfully serve and care
until they come to a happy end
in eternity with you

Mechthild of Magdeburg

Blessed are the poor in spirit for theirs is the
Kingdom of Heaven.
Blessed are they that mourn for they shall be comforted.
Blessed are the meek for they shall inherit the earth.
Blessed are those who do hunger and thirst after
righteousness for they shall be filled.
Blessed are the merciful for they shall obtain mercy.
Blessed are the poor in heart for they shall see God.
Blessed are the peacemakers for they shall be
called the children of God.
Blessed are they who are persecuted for righteousness'
sake, for theirs is the kingdom of Heaven.

Matthew 5: 3–10

*At times our own light goes out and is
rekindled by a spark from another person.
Each of us has cause to think with deep
gratitude of those who have lighted the flame
within us.*

ALBERT SCHWEITZER

My joy
My hunger
My shelter
My friend;
My food for the journey
My journey's End.

You are my breath,
My hope,
My companion,
My craving,
My abundant wealth.

Without You, my Life, my Love,
I would never have wandered across these
endless countries.
You have poured out so much grace for me,
Done me so many favours, given me so many gifts,
I look everywhere for Your love,
Then suddenly I am filled with it.

O Captain of my Heart
Radiant Eye of Yearning in my breast,
I will never be free from You
As long as I live.

Be satisfied with me, Love,
And I am satisfied.

Rabi'a

O Hidden Life, vibrant in every atom;
O Hidden Light, shining in every creature;
O Hidden Love, embracing all in Oneness;
May all who feel themselves as one with Thee,
Know they are therefore one with every other

Annie Besant

In Surrender

We live between the act of awakening and the act of surrender. Each morning, we awaken to the light and the invitation to a new day in the world of time; each night, we surrender to the dark to be taken to play in the world of dreams where time is no more.

JOHN O'DONOHUE

I will be truthful.
I will suffer no injustice.
I will be free from fear.
I will not use force.
I will be of good will to all men.

Mahatma Gandhi

Our Father, who art in heaven, Hallowed be Thy Name;
Thy kingdom come. Thy will be done on earth,
as it is in heaven.
Give us this day our daily bread.
And forgive us our trespasses, as we forgive those
who trespass against us.
And lead us not into temptation, but deliver us from evil.
Amen

The Lord's Prayer

Our Father

The Our Father contains all possible petitions; we cannot conceive of any prayer not already contained in it. It is to prayer what Christ is to humanity. It is impossible to say it once through, giving the fullest possible attention to each word, without a change, infinitesimal perhaps but real, taking place in the soul.

SIMONE WEIL

In the Hands of God

More than ever I find myself in the hands of God.
This is what I have wanted all my life from my youth.

But now there is a difference;
the initiative is entirely with God.

It is indeed a profound spiritual experience
to know and feel myself so totally in God's hands.

*Fr Pedro Arrupe, SJ (written after he was disabled by
a stroke and had to retire from all active ministry)*

Suscipe

Take, Lord, and receive all my liberty,
my memory, my understanding
and my entire will,
All I have and call my own.

You have given all to me.
To you, Lord, I return it.

Everything is yours; do with it what you will.
Give me only your love and your grace.
That is enough for me.

St Ignatius of Loyola

Prayer

Sr Mary Magdalen, Carmelites, Loughrea, Galway

Prayer! What is it?

First of all, prayer is what it always was: a lifting up of the mind and heart to God. For the Carmelite nun, St Teresa's definition means that it is friendly conversation with him whom we know loves us. Many people think of Mass as a time when we are at prayer, and since it is the best prayer of all why is there a decline in the numbers who go to Mass, especially among young people? We can try to explain it – but it may require as many explanations as there are people who no longer go to Mass.

So what is it about prayer? Very many people devote themselves to prayer; they can't seem to get along without it, and some even choose to devote their entire lives to the quest for the deepest prayer! Yet, there are others who never pray. Some have lapsed, some refuse to pray, some don't believe in prayer, seeing it as utter nonsense. Yet according to several surveys, those who continue to pray are among the most contented of people.

As a committed devotee, prayer has always been a part of my life. My mother was a great woman of prayer and, consciously and unconsciously, she passed it on to her family. In my life there has been an ebb and flow of prayer and sometimes it even seemed to disappear completely as I sought to go the ways of the world; thankfully, I never did lose this most precious gift.

Then one day I hearkened to God's irresistible inner voice and made the choice to live a life of prayer. It was only after experiencing the ups and downs of this life that I began to learn what prayer is all about. I thought I knew what I was doing only to discover I was simply handing myself over to God so that he could teach me how to pray. I was required to recite many prayers, to read others, and to endure others, but as God had given me the invitation he also gave me the training and painstakingly journeyed with me.

In Carmel I was introduced to the *Liturgy of the Hours*. The Liturgy of the Eucharist is known to many. Essentially, the liturgy is a dialogue between God and man: it puts into words the wishes and desires of the entire Christian people, making intercession for the needs common to all mankind. Christ himself intends that his prayer and sacrifice should continue throughout the ages in his Mystical Body, the Church. So the official prayer of the Church is the prayer that Christ addresses to the Father. *The Liturgy of the Hours* fosters dispositions of Faith, Hope and Love, devotion and a spirit of sacrifice. Christ is present when his community comes together, and both the sanctification of man and the worship of God are achieved by the setting up of a dialogue between God and man. In this way faith is nourished, minds are raised to God, and we are better disposed to receive his grace. As well as praising God, the Church's liturgy intercedes for the salvation of the whole world.

The next hurdle was to learn to recite the liturgical prayers well. Thus began the daily effort to cleanse my heart of vain evil and wandering thoughts, to enlighten my understanding and purify my will so that I might devoutly praise God. This was a daily discipline and a loving chore. A lifetime is not long enough to do it justice.

Lectio Divina, a vital adjunct to prayer, means reading the Scriptures and pondering them until they almost become a mirror in which ourselves, our lives and our world are reflected. We are then able to respond to God in prayer.

Prayer is an opening up to God. I learned to call out to God on behalf of others, for their needs, often so sad and urgent. I also prayed for my friends and for myself for I was full of faults. I prayed for priests and bishops and the Pope. Gradually, though slowly, prayer grew in me until it became more like a relationship with God. The wonderful sense of the presence of God could at times be overwhelming, and at other times just the absolute conviction that he was always there, deep within me so that to make contact I had only to look at the one who, as St Teresa says, never takes his eyes off me.

For the Carmelite nun, prayer and the practice of virtue are inseparable. St Teresa mentions three virtues in particular: love for one another, detachment and humility. She says that all the other virtues are included if we practise these three. To grow in the virtues is to grow in prayer. Ideally we learn to talk to God as a friend, and to speak to God in one's own words is indeed prayer; when one's whole life is prayer one keeps perfecting this dialogue with God; or rather, God keeps perfecting it in us. Prayer is simply talking to God and truly listening to him. Our lives and our words must speak the same language.

As this communication matures, something really beautiful for God and man comes to birth, unique to each individual. Here, Mary is the model par excellence. Just as Mary was especially chosen, so are we – each and every one of us. Like Mary, we have been given all the graces we needed. She lived a life of faith and hope blossoming into love for God and man. As we falter on our way we can gaze on Mary and gain the strength we need. Life is a battle, a really big testing of us. If we live it well the rewards are immense; if not, then the punishment is severe – because it is eternal. The safest way to that land of blessedness is to travel faithfully along the path of prayer.

The next step in my life of prayer was the discovery of a love story. What is true of human love is even more true of divine love.

His creature and I am caught up in this very mystery. I was beginning to understand what being married to God meant. Prayer is learning to fall in love with God. I was gradually moving towards living for him, but now I discovered how very fond I was of myself! So I had to start all over again, and every time I found myself I had to give that much more of myself to God. I am resolved to keep on trying until I die and it is in this trying that the mystery is resolved. I am weak and fragile, but the more I give myself to God the more I lose the selfish part of me that can never become a part of God. If every day I give a little more, then one day I will be totally given to God. I try to follow Christ as Mary did with total fidelity, a fidelity that can only come from God.

God within me, God without
How shall I ever be in doubt?
There is no place where I may go
And not there see God's face, not know
I am God's vision and God's ears,
So through the harvest of my years
I am the sower and the sown
God's self unfolding and God's own

From a 16th-century Celtic gravestone

If one descends into oneself
Then what is found
Is precisely what is desired

Simone Weil

The creative process is a process
of surrender, not control.

Julia Cameron

The symphony needs each note.
The book needs each word.
The house needs each brick.
The ocean needs each drop of water.
The harvest needs each grain of wheat.
The whole of humanity needs you
as and where you are.
You are unique.
No one can take your place.

Michel Quoist

The whole course of things goes to teach us faith. We need only obey. There is guidance for each of us, and by lowly listening we shall hear the right word . . . Place yourself in the middle of the stream of power and wisdom which flows into you as life, place yourself in the full center of that flood, then you are without effort impelled to truth, to right, and a perfect contentment.

RALPH WALDO EMERSON

When I rise up let me rise up
Joyful like a bird.
When I fall
Let me fall without regret
Like a leaf.

Wendell Berry

What is God?
God is?

Meister Eckhart

Father,
I abandon myself into your hands
Do with me what you will
Whatever you do I thank you
I am ready for all, I accept all
Let only your will be done in me

And in all your creatures
I wish no more than this, O Lord

Into your hands I commend my soul
I offer it to you
With all the love of my heart,
For I love you, Lord,
And so need to give myself
to surrender myself into your hands
Without reserve
And with boundless confidence
Because you are my father

Adapted from Charles de Foucauld, 'Prayer of Abandonment'

Each morning I stop
I stand
Feel the weight of feet on floor
Sinking into Mother Earth
Mother Earth is the symbol
Of the Lord holding me
In the palm of her hand
Mother Earth protects me
Gives me space to move
Gives me food and drink
And shelter
I offer Mother Earth gratitude
I imagine the Lord Jesus
Standing in front of me
Offering me peace
I surrender to the Lord Jesus
The past, present and future
Ask the Lord Jesus to give me his peace
To give me courage and compassion
And forgiveness and strength
For this new day
I ask him to lead me with the divine light
To the true path of union with the divine

Korko Moses

Generosity is giving more than you can and pride is taking less than you need

KAHLIL GIBRAN

God is a great underground river that no one can dam up and no one can stop

MEISTER ECKHART

God before me, God behind me,
God above me, God below me,
I on the path of God,
God upon my track.

A CELTIC PRAYER

Being is God's circle
And in this circle
All creatures exist
Everything that is in God
is God

Meister Eckhart

But now I have learned to listen to silence.
To hear its choirs singing the songs of ages,
Chanting the hymns of space, and disclosing
the secrets of eternity.

Kahlil Gibran

You have made us for yourself, oh Lord, and our hearts are restless until they rest in thee

Sᴛ Aᴜɢᴜsᴛɪɴᴇ

Start by doing what is necessary
Then do what is possible
And suddenly you are doing the impossible

St Francis of Assisi

Having Confessed

Let us lie down again
Deep in anonymous humility and God
May find us worthy material for His hand

Patrick Kavanagh

Prayer is freedom and affirmation
Growing out of nothingness with love
Prayer is the flowering of our innermost freedom
In response to the word of God
Prayer is not only dialogue with God
It is the communion of our freedom
With God's ultimate freedom
God's infinite spirit

Thomas Merton

Each thing I have received,
from Thee it came,
Each thing for which I hope,
from Thy love it will come,
Each thing I enjoy, it is of Thy bounty,
Each thing I ask comes of Thy disposing.

A CELTIC PRAYER

In Trust

Do not let your heart be troubled,
trust in God and trust in me.

JOHN 14: 1

Do not be afraid for I am with you.

ISAIAH 43: 5

The future enters into us
In order to transform itself in us
Long before it happens

Rainer Maria Rilke

Give me a sense of humour
Give me the grace to see a joke
To get some pleasure out of life
And pass it on to other folk

Anonymous

Only those who will risk going too far can possibly find out how far one can go.

T. S. Eliot

The sun will set without thy assistance

The Talmud

Prolong not the past
Invite not the future
Alter not your innate wakefulness
Don't fear appearances
There is nothing more than this

Tibetan Buddhism

Dear friend please know as you pass by
As you are now so once was I
As I am now so you will be
Prepare yourself to follow me

Gravestone unknown

Do not overlook tiny good actions, thinking they are of no benefit; even tiny drops of water in the end will fill a huge vessel.

BUDDHA

Although the life of a person is in a land full of thorns and weeds, there is always a space in which the good seed can grow. You have to trust God.

POPE FRANCIS

*My Lord God, I have no idea where I am going.
I do not see the road ahead of me. I cannot
know for certain where it will end. Nor do I
really know myself, and the fact that I think
that I am following your will does not mean
that I am actually doing so. But I believe that
the desire to please you does in fact please
you. And I hope I have that desire in all that I
am doing. I hope that I will never do anything
apart from that desire. And I know that if I do
this you will lead me by the right road though
I may know nothing about it. Therefore will I
trust you always though I may seem to be lost
and in the shadow of death. I will not fear, for
you are ever with me, and you will never
leave me to face my perils alone.*

THOMAS MERTON

Happiness is like a butterfly: the more you chase it, the more it will elude you; but if you turn your attention to other things, it will come and sit softly on your shoulder.

HENRY DAVID THOREAU

To dare is to lose one's footing momentarily.
Not to dare is to lose oneself.

Søren Kierkegaard

Have patience with everything unresolved in your heart
and try to love the questions themselves . . .
Don't search for the answers,
which could not be given to you now,
because you would not be able to live them.
And the point is, to live everything.
Live the questions now.
Perhaps then, someday far in the future,
you will gradually, without even noticing it,
live your way into the answer.

Rainer Maria Rilke

I truly believe that everything that we do and everyone that we meet is put in our path for a purpose. There are no accidents; we're all teachers – if we're willing to pay attention to the lessons we learn, trust our positive instincts and not be afraid to take risks or wait for some miracle to come knocking at our door.

MARLA GIBBS

To be alive and free you must shed your fear of walking unaccompanied

TONY DE MELLO

You may give them your love but not your thoughts,
For they have their own thoughts.
You may house their bodies but not their souls,
For their souls dwell in the house of tomorrow,
which you cannot visit, not even in your dreams.
You may strive to be like them,
but seek not to make them like you.
For life goes not backward nor tarries with yesterday.

Kahlil Gibran

God meets us right where we are,
'and lo I am with you always, even unto
the end of the world'

Matthew 28: 20

You keep those in perfect peace
whose minds are fixed on you,
because they trust in you . . .
Trust in the Lord for ever

Isaiah 26: 3–4

Our soul is waiting for the Lord.
He is our help and our shield.
In him do our hearts find joy.
We trust in his holy name.
May your love be upon us, O Lord,
as we place all our hope in you.

Psalm 33: 20–22

*All shall be well, and all manner
of things shall be well*

JULIAN OF NORWICH

*As soon as you trust yourself,
you will know how to live.*

JOHANN WOLFGANG VON GOETHE

Age is an opportunity no less
Than youth itself, though in another dress,
And as the evening twilight fades away
The sky is filled with stars, invisible by day

Henry Wadsworth Longfellow, 'Morituri Salutamus'

Rejoice always.
Pray without ceasing.
In everything give thanks.

I Thessalonians 5: 16–18

Prayer is the Most Human and Personal Thing We Do

Sr Bernardine Meskell, Poor Clares, Ennis, Co. Clare

The very heart and nourishment of our relationship with God is prayer. Prayer, as an act of turning towards God, is, or ought to be, the most natural thing we do – not just one of the things we do. It should fulfil the whole purpose of our being, get us in touch with our deepest reality. Prayer is the most human and personal thing we do. It is not just for 'professional contemplatives'. But we who are called to contemplative orders are in a plum position with all the privileges, graces and environment to dispose ourselves to receive the gift of contemplative prayer which is, after all, the greatest gift God gives us. And isn't it only right that there should be at least some people giving God their full attention? As Gerard Manley Hopkins said, Our Lady had 'this one work has to do – Let all God's glory through'.

Contemplatives may appear to be doing nothing. Yet Christ hung on the Cross for three hours, doing nothing. Still, those three hours were the supreme height of a love beyond comprehension. Those looking on urged him to come down from the Cross, as we are often urged to leave our prayerful solitude and do something. Christ did not move . . . Often when engaged in prayer or, as someone ironically described it to me, 'being physically present in the chapel at the time appointed for prayer', we may feel that we are doing nothing and would be as well off out in the garden mowing the lawn for the love of God. When you think about it, at mealtimes we can't actually see the beneficial effects food is having on our system, but if anyone's faith in the fact is wavering there is an easy way to put it to the test! Similarly, if I absent myself from prayer for just a few days, even for the best of reasons, I quickly realize that those seemingly blank half-hours are times of the most intense activity. If the vital force of silent contemplative prayer was suddenly withdrawn from the world, that world, not always conscious of its presence, would be acutely aware of its absence. Everything truly human finds a place in our hearts at prayer. We live in a world where there are many who yearn for direction, comfort, reassurance and prayerful support from those who live by listening to God, speaking with God and who are blessed to live hidden in the embrace of God.

As the bridegroom rejoices over the bride,
so shall your God rejoice over you

Isaiah 62: 5

Like a golden beacon signalling on a moonless night,
Tao guides our passage through this transitory realm.
In moments of darkness and pain
remember all is cyclical.
Sit quietly behind your wooden door:
Spring will come again.

Loy Ching-Yuen

God, bless Thou Thyself my reaping,
Each ridge, and plain, and field,
Each sickle curved, shapely, hard,
Each ear and handful on the sheaf.
Each ear and handful on the sheaf.

A CELTIC BLESSING

In Praise

*Glory be to him whose power, working in us,
can do infinitely more than we can ask or
imagine; glory be to him from generation
to generation in the Church and in
Christ Jesus for ever and ever. Amen.*

EPHESIANS 3: 14–21

O all you works of the Lord, O bless the Lord.
To him be highest glory and praise for ever.
And you, angels of the Lord, O bless the Lord.
To him be highest glory and praise for ever.

And you, the heavens of the Lord, O bless the Lord.
And you, clouds of the sky, O bless the Lord.
And you, all armies of the Lord, O bless the Lord.
To him be highest glory and praise for ever.

And you, sun and moon, O bless the Lord.
And you, the stars of the heav'ns, O bless the Lord.
And you, showers and rain, O bless the Lord.
To him be highest glory and praise for ever.

And you, all you breezes and winds, O bless the Lord.
And you, fire and heat, O bless the Lord.
And you, cold and heat, O bless the Lord.
To him be highest glory and praise for ever.

And you, showers and dew, O bless the Lord.
And you, frosts and cold, O bless the Lord.
And you, frost and snow, O bless the Lord.
To him be highest glory and praise for ever.

(*Continued*)

And you, night-time and day, O bless the Lord.
And you, darkness and light, O bless the Lord.
And you, lightning and clouds, O bless the Lord.
To him be highest glory and praise for ever.

O let the earth bless the Lord.
To him be highest glory and praise for ever.

And you, mountains and hills, O bless the Lord.
And you, all plants of the earth, O bless the Lord.
And you, fountains and springs, O bless the Lord.
To him be highest glory and praise for ever.

And you, rivers and seas, O bless the Lord.
And you, creatures of the sea, O bless the Lord.
And you, every bird in the sky, O bless the Lord.
And you, wild beasts and tame, O bless the Lord.
To him be highest glory and praise for ever.
And you, children of men, O bless the Lord.
To him be highest glory and praise for ever.
O Israel, bless the Lord, O bless the Lord
And you, priests of the Lord, O bless the Lord.
And you, servants of the Lord, O bless the Lord
To him be highest glory and praise for ever.

And you, spirits and souls of the just, O bless the Lord
And you, holy and humble of heart, O bless the Lord.
Ananias, Azarias, Mizael, O bless the Lord.
To him be highest glory and praise for ever.

Let us praise the Father, the Son, and Holy Spirit.
To you be highest glory and praise for ever.

May you be blessed, O Lord, in the heavens.
To you be highest glory and praise for ever.

The Canticle of Daniel – 3: 57–88

The heavens proclaim the glory of God
and the firmament shows forth the work of his hands.
Day unto day takes up the story
and night unto night makes known the message.

No speech, no word, no voice is heard
yet their span goes forth through all the earth,
their words to the utmost bounds of the world.

There he has placed a tent for the sun;
it comes forth like a bridegroom coming from his tent,
rejoices like a champion to run its course.

At the end of the sky is the rising of the sun;
to the furthest end of the sky is its course.
There is nothing concealed from its burning heat.

Psalm 19: 1–6

O God, you have formed Heaven and Earth
You have given me all the goods that the earth bears
Here is your part, my God, take it

Prayer from Zaire

OM this eternal word is all,
What was, what is, what shall be
And what beyond is in eternity
All is Om

The Upanishads

Thou my mother and my father thou
Thou my friend and my teacher thou
Thou my wisdom and my riches
Thou art all to me, O God of all Gods

An Indian prayer

Christ has no body now on earth but yours
Yours are the only hands with which he can do his work
Yours the only feet with which he can go about the world
Yours are the only eyes with which his compassion can
shine forth upon a troubled world
Christ has no body on earth now but yours

St Teresa of Avila

Holy Spirit,
Giving life to all life,
Moving all creatures,
Root of all things,
Washing them clean,
Wiping out their mistakes,
Healing their wounds,
You are our true life,
Luminous, wonderful,
Awakening the heart from its ancient sleep

Hildegard of Bingen, 12th-century abbess and mystic

And Mary said,
My soul magnifies the Lord,
And my spirit rejoices in God my Saviour.
He looks on his handmaid, in her lowliness
and henceforth all ages will call me blessed.
The almighty works marvels for me
Holy is his name
He mercy is from age to age on those who fear him
He has shown strength with his arm;
he scattererd the proud in their conceited hearts.
He put down the mighty from *their* thrones
and exalted the lowly.
He filled the hungry with good things;
and sent the rich away wealthy.

Luke 1: 46–49

How could they not bow down in love and adoration before thee, God of Gods, Spirit Supreme? Thou creator of Brahma, the God of creation, thou infinite, eternal, refuge of the world. Thou art all that is, and all that is not, and all that is beyond

BHAGAVAD GITA

Let the air and the ether praise you
Let the books and the letters praise you
Let the fish in the streams praise you
Let the thought and the action praise you
Let the sand grains and earth clods praise you
Let all the good that's performed praise you
And I shall praise you
Lord of joy, Glorious Lord
I give you greeting!

Gaelic benediction

I find you, Lord, in all Things and in all
my fellow creatures, pulsing with your life;
as a tiny seed you sleep in what is small
and in the vast you vastly yield yourself

Rainer Maria Rilke

He who is in the sun and in the fire and
in the heart of man is one.
He who knows this is one with the one

The Upanishads

I am bending my knee
In the eye of the Father who created me,
In the eye of the Son who purchased me,
In the eye of the Spirit who cleansed me,
In friendship and affection

Celtic rhyme

You, O eternal Trinity, are a deep sea into which the more I enter, the more I find, and the more I find, the more I seek … O abyss, O eternal God, O sea profound, what more could you give me than yourself? Amen

CATHERINE OF SIENA

Insults should be written in the sand, and praises carved in stone.

ARAB PROVERB

All you *big* things, bless the Lord.
Mount Kilimanjaro and Lake Victoria,
The Rift Valley and the Serengeti Plain,
Fat baobabs and shady mango trees,
All eucalyptus and tamarind trees,
Bless the Lord.
Praise and extol Him for ever and ever.

All you *tiny* things, bless the Lord.
Busy black ants and hopping fleas,
Wriggling tadpoles and mosquito larvae,
Flying locusts and water drops,
Pollen dust and tsetse flies,
Millet seeds and dried dagaa,
Bless the Lord.
Praise and extol Him for ever and ever.

East African canticle

You are the notes, we are the flute
We are the mountain, you are the sounds coming down
We are the pawns and kings and rooks
we set on a board: we win or we lose.
We are lions rolling and unrolling on flags.
Your invisible wind carries us through the world.

Rumi

I shall sing a praise to God:
Strike the chords upon the drum.
God who gives us all good things –
Strike the chords upon the drum –
Wives, and wealth, and wisdom.
Strike the chords upon the drum.

Prayer from Zaire

Glory to you for the feast-day of life,
Glory to you for the perfume of lilies and roses,
Glory to you for each different taste of berry and fruit,
Glory to you for the sparkling silver of
early morning dew,
Glory to you for the joy of dawn's awakening,
Glory to you for the new life each day brings

Gregory Petrov

The lark's on the wing;
The snail's on the thorn
God's in His heaven –
All's right with the world!

Robert Browning

Our Lord is great and almighty;
his wisdom can never be measured.
The Lord raises the lowly;
he humbles the wicked to the dust.
O sing to the Lord giving thanks;
sing psalms to our God with the harp.
He covers the heavens with clouds;
he prepares the rain for the earth,
making mountains sprout with grass
and with plants to serve man's needs.
He provides the beasts with their food
and young ravens that call upon him.
His delight is not in horses
nor his pleasure in warriors' strength.
The Lord delights in those who revere him,
in those who wait for his love.

Psalm 147: 5–11

The sacred Three
To save
To shield
To surround
the Heart
The House
The Household
This eve
This night
O! This eve
This night
and every night
Each single night
Amen

A CELTIC PRAYER

In Love

You know quite well, deep within you, that there is only a single magic, a single power, a single salvation . . . and that is called loving. Well, then, love your suffering. Do not resist it, do not flee from it. It is your aversion that hurts, nothing else.

HERMANN HESSE

If one is cruel to himself, how can we expect him to be compassionate with others?

HASDAI IBN SHAPRUT

For He is that very love which enwraps and enfolds us,
embraces us and guides us,
surrounds us with his love,
which is so tender,
that He may never desert us

Julian of Norwich

Love a man even in his sin, for that is the semblance of Divine Love and is the highest love on earth. Love all God's creation, the whole and every grain of sand in it. Love every leaf, every ray of God's light. Love the animals, love the plants, love everything. If you love everything, you will perceive the divine mystery in things. Once you perceive it, you will begin to comprehend it better every day. And you will come at last to love the whole world with an all-embracing love.

FYODOR DOSTOEVSKY, *THE BROTHERS KARAMAZOV*

Neither painting nor sculpting can any longer quieten my soul, turned now to that Divine love which on the cross, to embrace us, opened wide his arms

MICHELANGELO

Letter to Sister Stan

from Sr Marie Fahy
St Mary's Abbey
Glencairn
Co. Waterford

Thursday, 1 January 2015

Dear Sister Stan,

You asked me to share with you some reflections about my experience of prayer. So on this New Year's Day I thought I might at least begin these brief reflections and I hope you will be encouraged by this humble effort to respond to your request.

To be honest, my prayer is my life, and my life is my prayer.

I got a good start. I was raised in a faith culture at home, and in school the Mercy Sisters taught me how to pray. My First Communion and Confirmation days were truly experiences of God. I learned to trust the guiding inner spirit leading me to know and follow Christ Jesus. I've had a double share of religious and monastic vow celebrations. When I was 21, I made my first profession as an Incarnate Word Sister; seven years later my final vows. After years of formation, training and missionary work I transferred to the Cistercian community of Glencairn. While I greatly appreciated the outreach and work of the Incarnate Word Sisters, I felt this 'call within a call' to make a solemn commitment to prayer at the heart of the Church. And so I continued the spiritual journey to Solemn Profession and ten years later I was blessed as Abbess of the community. I will soon begin my fourteenth year as Abbess.

That is the broad context of my story. My relationship with the Lord has been marked by desire, struggle, support, grace, deepening and the inevitable Cross.

Inner desire is what has led me in the choices I've made and not made. I always had a sense that the Lord Jesus was the love of my life, and for this reason I was simply unmarriageable. I trusted the Lord to look after the minutest details of my life and my life was for his kingdom and mission.

Because of this I had to confront huge struggles

– family needs, independence, career, emotional and affective needs. The challenge to be conformed to Christ, to become spiritually and psychologically mature, to accept the deprivations of celibate life, was an ongoing struggle and effort. And many times I felt so like St Paul: 'I do not do the good I want, but the evil I do not want' (Rom. 7: 19).

But the Lord who can never be outdone in generosity always puts people at my side who give me immeasurable support, love, friendship and inspiration. Community members, work colleagues, spiritual directors, soul friends, retreat-givers, confessors and my good parents (RIP) and family members. I always felt loved by 'someone' even when I was struggling with various misunderstandings, tension in relationships, lack of zeal, and the temptation to give up. Somehow there was always someone there to keep me going on this straight and narrow path of following Christ Jesus.

Gradually, I came to understand the wonder of grace, the wonder of how God touches our emotions and understanding. I know from experience that God hears every human cry and every human effort to surrender to his grace and guidance. Grace has come to me through daily experiences, but mostly through prayer. While the significant moments of community prayer and daily Eucharist are vital, I also find God through my personal reading of the Scriptures, by talking out my feelings and questions in spiritual direction, listening to the reading in the refectory, hours of prayer in solitude, in the wonder of nature, or before the Blessed Sacrament. All this warms my heart and keeps me living in Christ and attentive to the grace of the indwelling Spirit of Christ.

The deepening of my trust in the indwelling Spirit of Christ and the Father's love has become my greatest security and gives me confidence and self-esteem. These are expressed in prayer. I notice this most when, in circumstances that could pull me in the opposite direction, I have enough inner strength and inner freedom to be loving, forgiving and compassionate. Another sign of deepening trust in God's providence and care is when I can live through difficult challenges and situations with peace and acceptance. It sometimes takes time but eventually the agitation subsides, light dawns and peace returns.

Faithfulness to daily prayer in any form does not exempt us from the trials and suffering that are simply part of living. I make mistakes; these poor choices bring suffering to others; without intending to, I sometimes forget to affirm the people around me; things don't work out as I think they should. Bringing these situations to the Lord in prayer helps me to live through them and face them with a new strength, with the confidence of Jesus in his Father even as he faced his crucifixion. Many times my prayer is simply: With Christ I die upon the Cross. My dying is usually to self-will – selfishness in one form or another – to the false self. And with Christ my rising is to new life, to more humanity, more compassion, more dependence on God's grace and spirit.

Though there is such huge richness in Scripture there are passages which I have inhabited more frequently and which continue to give me strength and direction. I would like to share a few of these with you:

I believe nothing can happen that will outweigh the
supreme advantage of knowing Christ Jesus my Lord.
(Phil. 3: 8)

Make your home in me as I make mine in you.
(John 15: 4)

*I have loved you with an everlasting love and I am constant
in my affection for you.* (Jer. 31: 3)

*But now, thus says Yahweh . . . Do not be afraid for I
have redeemed you; I have called you by your name
you are mine. Should you pass through the sea I will be
with you; or through rivers they will not swallow you
up . . . You are precious in my eyes, because you are
honoured and I love you.* (Isa. 43: 1–4)

*. . . even there your hand would lead me, your
right hand would hold me fast.* (Ps. 138: 7)

My dear Sister Stan, you may have the impression
that my prayer is focused only on myself! This is not
my experience. Prayer liberates me, moves me to go
out to others in love, tenderness and support. When I
find myself becoming frustrated and impatient I know
it is time to step back and rest in the Lord, inhabit
the Scriptures and renew my union with the Spirit of
Christ. Sometimes the frustration just melts. The Lord
does take away the afflictive emotion; then I can be
kind naturally and with little effort. I wonder if this is
the Joy Pope Francis talks about in his exhortation on
Consecrated Life?

Much of my prayer is intercessory prayer for others . . . for so many needs. I believe that the Holy Spirit carries all our groans, all our wordless needs, to the Father. When we join our voices with the voice of Christ saying 'Abba Father' all the needs and sufferings of others and of our times are brought to the Father for healing, strength and transformation, and our prayer is heard. 'During his life on earth, Jesus offered up prayer and entreaty, aloud and in silent tears, to the one who had the power to save him out of death, and he submitted so humbly that his prayer was heard' (Hab. 5: 7).

As we move through the Mysteries of Christ's life in the seasons and feasts of the year I am nourished and motivated for prayer. My contemplative moments and insights always seem to come from the liturgy. I suppose the combination of music, word and atmosphere brings us to experience the touch of God.

I feel very privileged to be in this place, to be upheld by the good zeal of those around me, and to be in prayer for our Church and our fragile world.

With my warmest good wishes,
Sister Marie Fahy

The Kingdom of God is within you

LUKE 17: 21

You can search throughout the entire universe for someone who is more deserving of your love and affection than you are yourself, and that person is not to be found anywhere. You yourself, as much as anybody in the entire universe deserve your love and affection.

BUDDHA

Nothing is more practical than finding God,
than falling in Love
in a quite absolute, final way.
What you are in love with,
what seizes your imagination,
will affect everything.
It will decide
what will get you out of bed in the morning,
what you do with your evenings,
how you spend your weekends,
what you read,
whom you know,
what breaks your heart,
and what amazes you
with joy and gratitude.
Fall in Love,
stay in love,
and it will decide everything

Fr Pedro Arrupe, SJ

*Perhaps everything that frightens us is,
in its deepest essence, something helpless
that wants our love*

RAINER MARIA RILKE, *LETTERS TO A YOUNG POET*

She whom we love and lose
Is no longer where she was before.
She is now wherever we are

St John Chrysostom

As the father has loved me,
so have I loved you

JOHN 15: 9

I led you with reins of kindness, with leading
strings of love, I was like someone who lifts an
infant close against his cheek. Stooping down
to you I gave you food. How could I part
with you? How could I give you up?

HOSEA 11: 4 & 8

The Sowing of Meanings

For like a grain of fire
Smouldering in the heart
Of every living essence
God plants his undivided power
Buries his thought too vast
For worlds
In seeds and roots
And blade and flower

Thomas Merton

It is only with the heart that one can see rightly; what is essential is invisible to the eye

ANTOINE DE SAINT-EXUPÉRY, *THE LITTLE PRINCE*

Be kind whenever it is possible.
It is always possible.

HH THE DALAI LAMA

For, lo, the winter is past, the rain is over and gone;
The flowers appear on the earth; the time
of the singing of birds is come

Song of Songs 2: 10

Keep love in your heart. A life without it is like a sunless garden when the flowers are dead.

OSCAR WILDE

For Mercy has a human heart,
Pity a human face,
And Love the human form divine,
And Peace the human dress

William Blake, 'The Divine Image'

Forget my bones
Keep my spirit

St Kieran, 5th-century Irish saint

Love feels no burden, thinks nothing of trouble, attempts what is above its strength, pleads no excuse of impossibility; for it thinks all things lawful for itself, and all things possible

THOMAS À KEMPIS

Anyone without a soul-friend is like a body without a head.

ST BRIGID

In the morning
God and I meet together
To exchange our compassion and aspiration
In the evening
God and I meet together
To exchange our forgiveness and gratitude

Sri Chinmoy

To gladden the heart of a human being
To feed the hungry
To help the afflicted
To lighten the sorrow of the sorrowful
To remove the wrongs of the injured
That person is the most beloved of God
who does most good to God's creatures

Prophet Muhammad

The hunger for love is much more difficult to remove than the hunger for bread.

MOTHER TERESA

Love and compassion are necessities, not luxuries. Without them humanity cannot survive.

HH THE DALAI LAMA

Each one of us possesses a divine spark
However not everyone brings it to light
as fully as possible
The spark is like a diamond
The latter cannot spread radiance if it is
hidden in the earth
But each one of us contain the light as from a diamond
As soon as we make it shine in the suitable setting

Hasidic wisdom

Love is not concerned
with how you pray
Or where you slept
the night you ran away
from home
Love is concerned
that the beating of your heart
Should kill no one

Alice Walker

God respects me when I work;
but God loves me when I sing

Rabindranath Tagore

O love, O pure deep love, be here,
be now – be all;
Worlds dissolve into your stainless
endless radiance,
Frail living leaves burn with you
brighter than cold stars.
Make me your servant, your breath,
your core.

Rumi

I pray not for wealth
I pray not for honours
I pray not for pleasure,
Or even the joys of poetry
I only pray that during all my life
I may have love,
That I may have pure love to love thee

Chaitanya

Like the bird
That gazes all night
At the passing moon,
I have lost myself dwelling in You.
O my Beloved –
Return

Mirabai

My life is an instant
My life a fleeting hour
A moment in time
which escapes and is no more
I have only today to love you, Lord

St Thérèse of Lisieux

Waking up this morning, I smile.
Twenty-four brand new hours are before me.
I vow to live fully in each moment
And to look at all beings with the eyes of compassion.

Thich Nhat Hanh

I slept and dreamt that life was all joy.
I awoke and saw that life was but service.
I served and understood that service was joy.

Rabindranath Tagore

Lord, you are my lover,
My longing,
My flowing stream,
My sun,
And I am your reflection

Mechthild of Magdeburg

O Lord help me not to despise or oppose
what I do not understand

WILLIAM PENN

Love is always patient and kind; love is never
jealous; love is not boastful or conceited.
It is never rude and never seeks its own
advantage, it does not take offence
or store up grievances.
Love does not rejoice at wrongdoing,
but finds its joy in the truth.
It is always ready to make allowances, to trust,
to hope and to endure whatever comes.
Love never comes to an end.

I CORINTHIANS 13: 4–8/9

How would it be
If just for today
we thought less about contests
and rivalries, profits and politics,
winners and losers
And more about helping and giving,
mending and blending,
reaching out and pitching in.
How would it be?

Anonymous

Like the deer that yearns
for flowing streams,
so my soul is longing
for you, my God.
My soul is thirsting for God,
the Living God;
when can I enter and see
the face of God?

Psalm 42

Prayer of Longing

O thou who art at home
Deep in my heart
Enable me to join you
Deep in my heart

The Talmud

God sees with merciful eyes
Not what you are
Or what you have been
But what you desire to be

The Cloud of Unknowing

When I learned to read God's word in the book of my everyday life, then I became aware of a continuity and wholesome integrity of all that I do in the course of the day. Everything promises to be an encounter with God. My sacred reading, my work, the liturgical prayer, the interaction with others. My appreciation of nature, music and art. Everything becomes a way through which the Word of God speaks to me.

St Bernard of Clairvaux

God is and always will be Mystery — only a non-arguing presence, only a non-assertive self, can possibly have the humility and honesty to receive such mysterious silence.

When you can remain at peace inside of your own mysterious silence you are only beginning to receive the immense 'Love that moves the sun and the other stars' as Dante so beautifully says — God is always found at the depths, even at the depth of our sin and brokenness. And in the depths it is silent.

RICHARD RORH

Our actions have a tongue of their own. They have an eloquence of their own, even when the tongue is silent. For deeds prove the love more than words.

St Cyril of Jerusalem

Being a Christian isn't just following commandments. It means being in Christ. Acting like him, loving like him. It means letting him take possession of our lives and changing them, transforming them, freeing them from the darkness of evil.

Pope Francis

Lord I believe, help Thou my unbelief. My faith may be the size of a mustard seed, but even so, even aside from its potential, it brings with it a beginning of love, an inkling of love so intense that human love with all its heights and depths pales in comparison.

DOROTHY DAY

We need to love our neighbour, not just because he is pleasant or helpful or rich or influential or even because he shows us gratitude. These motives are too self-serving . . . Genuine love rises above creatures and soars up to God. In him, by him and through him it loves all men, both good and wicked, friends and enemies.

ST MAXIMILIAN KOLBE

For Serenity

In my young days I never tasted sorrow.
I wanted to become a famous poet.
I wanted to get ahead so I pretended to be sad
Now I am old and have known the
depth of every sorrow,
And I am contented to loaf
And enjoy the clear autumn

Hsin Ch'i-Chi, 'To an Old Tune'

The outer man is the swinging door
The inner man is the still hinge

Meister Eckhart

The deeper that sorrow carves into your being,
the more joy you can contain.
Is not the cup that holds your wine the very cup
that was burned in the potter's oven?

Kahlil Gibran

Serenity Prayer

God grant me the serenity
to accept the things I cannot change;
courage to change the things I can;
and wisdom to know the difference.

Living one day at a time;
enjoying one moment at a time . . .
as it is, not as I would have it;
trusting that He will make all things right
if I surrender to His Will

Reinhold Niebuhr

Every breath we take, every step we make, can be filled with peace, joy and serenity.

THICH NHAT HANH

True greatness lies not always
In the winning of worldly fame,
Nor doing our best spurred on by the cheers
And plaudits that follow our name.
But he who can face with a cheery grace
The everyday of life,
With its petty things that rasp and sting,
Is a hero in the strife

Fannie Herron Wingate

Finish each day and be done with it. You have done what you could. Some blunders and absurdities no doubt crept in; forget them as soon as you can. Tomorrow is a new day. You shall begin it serenely and with too high a spirit to be encumbered with your old nonsense

RALPH WALDO EMERSON

Let nothing disturb you,
Let nothing frighten you,
All things are passing away:
God never changes.
Patience obtains all things
Whoever has God lacks nothing;
God alone suffices

St Teresa of Avila

Learning lessons is a little like reaching maturity. You're not suddenly more happy, wealthy, or powerful, but you understand the world around you better, and you're at peace with yourself. Learning life's lessons is not about making your life perfect, but about seeing life as it was meant to be.

ELISABETH KÜBLER-ROSS

Always we hope someone else has the answer
Some other place will be better
Some other time it will all turn out
This is it;
No one else has the answer, no other place will be better
and it has already turned out.
At the centre of your being you have the answer;
You know who you are
and you know what you want.
There is no need to run outside for better seeing.
Nor to peer from a window.
Rather abide at the centre of your being;
for the more you leave it, the less you learn.
Search your heart and see, the way to do is to be.

Lao Tzu

*Nothing in all creation is so like
God as stillness*

MEISTER ECKHART

If I am going to die, the best way to prepare
is to quiet my mind, and open my heart.
If I am going to live, the best way to prepare
is to quiet my mind, and open my heart

Ram Dass

If a man does not keep pace with his companions,
Perhaps it is because he hears a different drummer
Let him step to the music he hears,
However near or far away

Henry David Thoreau

All things are passing
Nothing is permanent
The seas come and go
The trees come and go
The birds come and go
The mountains come and go
The earth comes and goes
The creation comes and goes
The breath comes and goes
People come and go
The body comes and goes
The mind comes and goes
Only what is essential remains
What is essential is not visible
To the sense or mind
Only the essence remains
Only the essence is permanent
Only there I find my rest

Sr Stan

The Earth does not belong to man; Man belongs to the Earth. This we know. All things are connected like the blood which unites one family. Whatever befalls the Earth befalls the sons of the Earth. Man did not weave the web of life, he is merely a strand in it. Whatever he does to the web, he does to himself.

CHIEF SEATTLE

What I dream of is an art of balance, of purity and serenity devoid of troubling or depressing subject matter – a soothing, calming influence on the mind, rather like a good armchair which provides relaxation from physical fatigue.

HENRI MATISSE

A human being is part of a whole, called by us the 'Universe' — a part limited in time and space. He experiences himself, his thoughts, and feelings as something separated from the rest — a kind of optical delusion of his consciousness. This delusion is a kind of prison for us, restricting us to our personal desires and to affection for a few persons nearest us. Our task must be to free ourselves from this prison by widening our circles of compassion to embrace all living creatures and the whole of nature in its beauty.

ALBERT EINSTEIN, THE EINSTEIN PAPERS

*The outward freedom that we shall attain
will only be in exact proportion to the
inward freedom to which we may have
grown at a given moment. And if this is a
correct view of freedom, our chief energy
must be concentrated on achieving reform
from within.*

MAHATMA GANDHI

*Human beings, by changing the inner attitudes
of their minds, can change the
outer aspects of their lives.*

WILLIAM JAMES

Why should I feel discouraged
Why should the shadows come
Why should my heart feel lonely
And long for heaven and home
When Jesus is my portion
My constant friend is he
His eye is on the sparrow
and I know he watches me
I sing because I am happy
I sing because I am free
His eye is on the sparrow
and I know he watches me

African American spiritual

To be full of things is to be empty of God.
To be empty of things is to be full of God.

Meister Eckhart

Money can buy a bed but not sleep
Books but not brains
Food but not appetite
Finery but not beauty
A house but not a home
Medicine but not health
Luxuries but not culture
Amusement but not happiness
Religion but not salvation
A passport to everywhere but heaven

Henry David Thoreau

Our time here is in the present moment
To live in the present moment is a miracle
The miracle is not to walk on water
The miracle is to walk on the earth
In the present moment
To appreciate the peace and beauty
That are available now

Thich Nhat Hanh

Make yourself familiar with the angels and behold them frequently in spirit; for without being seen, they are present with you

St Francis de Sales

The Lord travels in all directions at once. The Lord arrives from all directions at once. Wherever we are, we find that he has just departed, wherever we go we find that he has just arrived before us.

Thomas Merton

The Contemplative Life

Anne Marie Maguire

The contemplative tradition echoes back through many centuries of spiritual wisdom from the early Christian saints such as the Desert Fathers and Mothers, St Bernard, St John of the Cross, St Teresa of Avila, Julian of Norwich and Meister Eckhart. It has been brought to us more recently by the writings of Thomas Merton, Henri Nouwen, Fr Thomas Keating, Fr Richard Rohr, James Finley, Fr Daniel J. O'Leary, Fr James Martin, and the rich heritage of modern writers and living 'saints'.

According to Thomas Merton, contemplation is 'awakening, enlightenment and the amazing intuitive grasp by which love gains certitude of God's creative and dynamic intervention in our daily life'. While we traditionally associate the contemplative life with cloistered monks and nuns, more and more laypeople are seeking balance through a gentler, contemplative context for their ordinary lives, whether they are parents, teachers or quantum physics professors. Such people yearn for a true authentic experience of life, even within the busy-ness of this modern world. Prayer, by creating an anchor in the heart, transforms our interior landscape to create a true and meaningful life, as exemplified by the contemplative Sisters at St Mary's Cistercian Abbey in Glencairn, Co. Waterford.

Monastic life at the Abbey moves through each day with the rhythm of the Divine Office: the community gathers for prayer in the Abbey Church seven times daily, in addition to the morning celebration of Mass. The Divine Office begins with Vigils at 4.10 a.m., and is completed by the community's evening gathering at Compline at around 7.55 p.m., to close the day once again in prayer. The office itself consists of the prayerful singing of psalms and hymns as well as readings from the Bible and moments of silence. Vigils is followed by a period of silent prayer, reading, and *Lectio Divina*, the sacred reading of the Bible. There are two periods of work daily except on Sundays; this enables the Abbey to run in a self-sufficient manner, including its Eucharistic Bread and Greeting Card businesses. In addition, a myriad of domestic and farm maintenance activities are carried out each day in a spirit of devotion to God and in a context of prayer and surrender to the Divine.

Throughout this rhythm, apart from the praying of the Divine Office and Mass, from rising in the early hours of the morning to the setting of the day, the community remains largely silent, bringing its attention, time and time again, interiorly to God. Devotion to contemplation and prayer leads the Sisters to a deeper experience of Presence, and to being internally 'united to all'. Vigils takes place at a time when people wake from sleep, often with troubles and worries. It is all too easy to forget that these concerns are held daily in prayer by the Sisters and in the prayer lives of all monastic traditions.

Sister Michele of St Mary's told me of her initial unexpected encounter with God at the age of eighteen: it ingrained in her a lifelong recognition of Presence and an unquenchable desire to remain there continually:

I had a wonderful sense of his Presence. He showed himself in his incredible beauty and love and I understood without a shadow of doubt that he was Love and that I was loved unconditionally and lifted up into that selfsame love.

This experience confirmed in her a deep knowing that the meaning of her life was to devote herself to this love, and soon thereafter she joined a religious missionary congregation. While her younger years as a nun saw her serving as a missionary nurse overseas, she eventually followed the deeper call to a life of contemplation, and some twenty-eight years ago joined the monastic life at St Mary's.

Father Thomas Keating, the Cistercian monk who rekindled meditation and brought us the Centering Prayer, tells us that 'the Spirit prays in us and we consent'. It is not just through formal prayers, or the praying of the Divine Office, or even *Lectio Divina* that prayer happens – prayer is a way of being. As the French Cistercian Abbot, André Louf, said, the objective of the monastic life is to awaken the heart and 'make it aware of that prayer which is always going on within it . . . It abides there.' Prayerfulness is a landscape that is continuously present around monastics and laypeople alike. The heart is prayed into Being:

There is a place in every man where God touches him and where he himself is constantly in contact with God. This is simply because at every instant God holds us in being. The place where this creative contact with God takes place is deep within me. If I can reach it I can touch God.

Following the Rule of St Benedict, the working day flows from more meditative prayer into the active daily chores. For most of this silent work time the Sisters continue to rest in Presence during their activities and 'Pray continually' (1 Thess. 5: 17). All daily events and encounters become devoted to this relationship with God, with Love. It is a discipline of seeing every moment as a gift from God, surrendering one's own self to the greater Self of God.

The call and grace of monastic life is to move from the superficial self to the deeper self and to live from the heart. The call is to listen to the voice of the Lord, moment by moment, and to make choices that are motivated by a surrender to God and his will.

Sr Marie, Abbess of
St Mary's Cistercian Abbey, Glencairn

In yielding, receiving and responding to God, at times there is a felt awareness of the presence of Divine energy; at others it is simply a patient knowing that

God is present. Contemplation strengthens both this awareness and the certainty that God is in everyone and in everything. Presence envelops our atmosphere, our surroundings, our personalities, our work and our life experiences. By following our heartfelt desires, planted there by God, by being and becoming fully ourselves, we respond.

The singing of the Psalms at the Divine Office, like the periods of quiet prayer and *Lectio Divina*, keeps the Sisters in touch with God and the concerns of others. Many people contact the Abbey and report answers and resolutions to their prayers, often in unexpected, yet welcome, ways. Through prayer, the Sisters know that even in the midst of difficulty, suffering, confusion, and even joys and breakthroughs, they are contained in the Love of God.

Inspired by the lives of the saints and by the Cistercian brotherhood throughout the centuries, one Sister felt her calling was deeply influenced by the example of St Joseph, with his unassuming protection, strength and hidden presence. Having spent thirty-two years as a missionary nun, she chose to follow her deeper yearning for the Cistercian life:

The Cistercian Way in its simplicity of lifestyle, in humble
manual labour and highly organized life, opens my heart to
discover and receive the ever-loving Presence of God
in the ordinary; in the obscure minute moments.

Sr Denise, St Mary's Cistercian Abbey

In day-to-day life in Glencairn, prayer is lived out in
the relationships within the Abbey community, and
with the wider community beyond. Harmony in the
Sisters' prayer life creates and nourishes harmonious
relationships, which then feed and nourish the prayer
life and direct it into yet deeper contemplation.
Community living fosters the Sisters' development
of deep compassion, forgiveness, tolerance and
understanding of their own perceived weaknesses
and failings, and those of others. This is humility.
St Bernard described the aim of the journey towards
humility as arriving at a 'no-self', which for him was
union with God in Love. His advice to 'return to your
own heart' was intended to bring people home to
where God dwells. A natural selflessness arises from
humility, and the generosity to perform hidden acts
of kindness and help for others. Prayer transforms the
heart into ever-increasing contentment.

As a layperson I have felt very drawn to the contemplative way, especially by the sense of an interior prayer that is constantly going on within me, even before I do anything – I am being prayed into Being. In our busy modern lives of external stimulation and demands, more and more people feel anxious, powerless and disillusioned. Mahatma Gandhi said that prayer is not asking; it is a longing of the soul – a daily admission of one's weakness. 'It is better in prayer to have a heart without words than words without a heart.'

I feel that the deepest aches and joys of the heart are always heard, especially those that defy words. Sometimes just being heard is enough. At others, simply allowing the interior ache to exist brings untold relief. Or we may have to practise a patient unknowing until some sense of resolution eventually comes.

Over time, through surrender and trust, I have gained more patience and tolerance for vulnerability and unknowing, and a wonder at the harmony with which each new situation becomes resolved, too often in spite of me. Such contemplative experiences have confirmed with unshakeable certainty that Life, that Love, that God is present in them.

One of the strange laws of the contemplative life is that in it you do not sit down and solve problems: you bear with them until they somehow solve themselves.
Or until life itself solves them for you.

THOMAS MERTON

Bibliography

Paul Diemer, *Love Without Measure: Extracts from the Writings of St Bernard of Clairvau*, Darton, Longman and Todd Ltd., 1990.

Thomas Keating OCSO, *Open Mind, Open Heart*, Bloomsbury, London, 2006.

André Louf, *The Cistercian Way, Cistercian Studies Series: Number Seventy-Six*, 1983/1989.

Thomas Merton, *The Inner Experience*, SPCK Publishing, 2003.

Thomas Merton, *New Seeds of Contemplation*, New Directions, 1972 and 2007.

Henri J. M. Nouwen, *The Genesee Diary*, Doubleday, 1976.

When we have broken our god of tradition, and ceased from our god of rhetoric, then may God fire the heart in his presence

RALPH WALDO EMERSON

Invited or not, God is present

CARL JUNG

Worship in the temple of the present moment

TONY DE MELLO

*Remember, we are all affecting the world
every moment, whether we mean to or not.
Our actions and states of mind matter,
because we're so deeply interconnected
with one another. Working on our own
consciousness is the most important thing
that we are doing at any moment, and being
love is the supreme creative act.*

RAM DASS

*Search your heart and see the
way to do is to be*

LAO TZU

We who lived in concentration camps can remember the men who walked through the huts comforting others, giving away their last piece of bread. They may have been few in number, but they offer sufficient proof that everything can be taken from a man but one thing: the last of the human freedoms — to choose one's attitude in any given set of circumstances, to choose one's own way

VIKTOR E. FRANKL, MAN'S SEARCH FOR MEANING

For Protection

Be Thou a bright flame before me,
Be Thou a guiding star above me,
Be Thou a smooth path below me,
Be Thou a kindly shepherd behind me,
Today, tonight and for ever more.

Prayer of St Columba

May the god of gentleness be with you,
Caressing you with sunlight and rain and wind.
May his tenderness shine through you,
To warm all who are hurt and lonely
May the blessing of gentleness be upon you

An Irish blessing

Lead, Kindly Light, amid the encircling gloom,
Lead me Thou on;
The night is dark, and I am far from home,
Lead Thou me on.
Keep Thou my feet, I do not ask to see
The distant scene, one step enough for me.
I was not ever thus, nor pray'd that Thou
Shouldst lead me on;
I loved to choose and see my path, but now
Lead Thou me on.
I loved the garish day, and spite of fears,
Pride ruled my will: remember not past years.

So long Thy power hath blest me, sure it still
Will lead me on.
O'er moor and fen, o'er crag and torrent, till
the night is gone,
And with the morn those angel faces smile,
Which I have loved long since and lost awhile.

John Henry Newman

Come to me all who labour and are heavy laden
and I will give you rest . . .
For my yoke is easy and my burden light

MATTHEW 11: 28 & 30

Lead us from darkness to the light
Lead us from illusion to wisdom
Lead us from death to deathlessness
Lead us from conflict and suffering
To harmony, peace and happiness

The Upanishads

May I possess the patience of the turtle
May I possess the wisdom of the owl
May I possess the loyalty of the dog
May I possess the smile of the Buddha
In every moment of my fortunate life

Randy Baron

Every morning when I wake,
Dear Lord, a little prayer I make,
O please do keep Thy lovely eye
On all poor creatures born to die

Child's prayer

Now I lay me down to sleep
Lord I pray my soul do keep
And if I die before I wake
Lord I pray my soul to take

Child's prayer

Do not overlook negative actions merely because they are small; however small a spark may be, it can burn down a haystack as big as a mountain

BUDDHA

Make us worthy, Lord, to serve those people throughout the world who live and die in poverty and hunger. Give them, through our hands, this day their daily bread and by our understanding love, give them peace and joy

MOTHER TERESA

If, at the beginning and end of our lives we depend on others' kindness, why then in the middle should we not act kindly towards others?

HH The Dalai Lama

O our Father, the Sky, hear us
and make us strong.
O our Mother, the Earth, hear us
and give us support.
O Spirit of the East,
send us your Wisdom.
O Spirit of the South,
may we walk your path of life.
O Spirit of the West,
may we always be ready for the long journey.
O Spirit of the North, purify us
with your cleansing winds.

A Sioux prayer

I cannot dance,
O Lord, unless You lead me.
If you wish me to leap joyfully, let me see You dance,
Let me see You dance joyfully,
Let me see You dance and sing.
Then I will leap into Love and from Love into
Knowledge,
from Knowledge into the Harvest,
That sweetest Fruit beyond human sense.
There I will stay with You, Whirling.

Mechthild of Magdeburg, translated by Jane Hirshfield (1994)

Spirit of the living God fall fresh on me
Spirit of the living God fall fresh on me
Melt me, mold me, fill me, use me,
Spirit of the living God fall fresh on me

Daniel Iverson

Lord, make me an instrument of Your peace;
Where there is hatred, let me sow love;
Where there is injury, pardon;
Where there is doubt, faith;
Where there is despair, hope;
Where there is darkness, light;
And where there is sadness, joy.
O Divine Master, Grant that I may not so much seek
To be consoled as to console;
To be understood as to understand;
To be loved as to love.
For it is in giving that we receive;
It is in pardoning that we are pardoned;
And it is in dying that we are born again to eternal life.

St Francis of Assisi

Make me pure: Lord, thou art holy;
Make me meek, Lord: thou wert lowly

Gerard Manley Hopkins

May the words of my mouth
and the meditation that is in my heart
be acceptable to thee, O Lord,
my strength and my redeemer

A Jewish prayer

God help us to live slowly:
To move simply:
To look softly:
To allow emptiness:
To let the heart create for us.
Amen

Michael Leunig

Christ be with me

Christ before me

Christ behind me

Christ in me

Christ beneath me

Christ above me

Christ on my right

Christ on my left

Christ when I lie down

Christ when I sit down

Christ when I rise

Christ in the heart of everyone

Who thinks of me

Christ in the mouth of everyone

Who speaks of me

Christ in every eye that seeks me

Christ in every ear that hears me

St Patrick

Hail, Holy Queen

Hail, holy Queen, Mother of mercy, hail, our life, our sweetness and our hope. To thee do we cry, poor banished children of Eve: to thee do we send up our sighs, mourning and weeping in this vale of tears. Turn then, most gracious Advocate, thine eyes of mercy toward us, and after this our exile, show unto us the blessed fruit of thy womb, Jesus. O clement, O loving, O sweet Virgin Mary! Pray for us, O Holy Mother of God, That we may be made worthy of the promises of Christ

Hail Mary

Hail Mary, full of grace. The Lord is with thee.
Blessed art thou amongst women,
and blessed is the fruit of thy womb, Jesus.
Holy Mary, Mother of God,
pray for us sinners,
now and at the hour of our death
Amen

Oh Angel of God, my Guardian dear, to whom His love commits me here, ever this day (or night) be at my side, to light and guard, to rule and guide. Amen

PRAYER TO GUARDIAN ANGEL

Keep me as the apple of your eye, hide me under the shadow of your wings

PSALM 17: 8

Memorare

Remember, O most gracious Virgin Mary,
that never was it known that anyone who
fled to your protection,
implored your help or sought your intercession,
was left unaided.
Inspired with this confidence,
I fly to you, O Virgin of virgins, my Mother;
to you do I come, before you I stand,
sinful and sorrowful.

O Mother of the Word Incarnate,
despise not my petitions,
but in your mercy hear and answer me.

Amen

Let the morning bring me word of your unfailing love,
for I have put my trust in you.
Show me the way I should go,
for to you I entrust my life.

Psalm 143: 8

Grant me to recognise in others, Lord God,
the radiance of your own face

Pierre Teilhard de Chardin, SJ

For Faith

Faith is to believe what you do not see; the reward of this faith is to see what you believe.

St Augustine

What Does Prayer Mean To Me?

Sr Regina McHugh, Poor Clares, Ennis, Co. Clare

Prayer is an awareness of God's loving presence in my life. It is the realization that God is closer to me than I ever imagined. Prayer helps me to be attentive to 'the Loving Divine Presence' in which I already exist. Prayer gives life and meaning to the passage in Acts 17: 28: 'In him we live, and move, and have our being.'

God is not 'out there'. We are already 'in God'. To quote St Catherine of Siena, 'As the fish is in the ocean and the ocean is in the fish, so we are in God. It is as if we are the fish swimming in the ocean of Divine Love.' God is like the air we breathe. That is why the deeper we grow in prayerful awareness of the Divine presence in our lives, the less we actually use words and the more we simply live it.

Thomas Merton gave very wise advice to an over-zealous beginner: 'How does an apple ripen? It just sits in the sun!' And just so is the life of prayer – sitting in the sun of the love of God to ripen in relationship. Prayer is not actively doing things to 'get' God. It is the awareness of basking in and breathing in the Divine presence.

Most people know the story told by John Vianney of the old man who, when asked by a priest what he did when he visited the church every day, replied, 'I sit here and look at Him and He looks at me. That's all.' But that's everything: loving attentiveness is the response we must offer to the one who is sharing. In prayer I am not actively searching for God. It is, rather, disposing myself to discover that I have already been found by God. It is becoming aware of his 'unconditional love' for me at every moment of my existence. This fills me with awe and reverence. God knows that I am here and I am his 'beloved'.

If I want to grow close to someone I want to spend time with them. This also applies to my growing relationship with Jesus. My deepest knowledge of Jesus is found in prayer. There he takes possession of me and shows me who he is. In my daily listening to him, in the silence of my heart and in the reading of sacred Scripture I allow God to mould me into the likeness of his Son. This guides the rhythm of my days. I endeavour to live 'prayerfully'. As Jesus tells us, 'If you make my word your home, you will indeed be my disciples. You will learn the truth and the truth will set you free' (John 8: 31–2). When I pray, the spirit prays in me. Prayer knows no boundaries – it reaches to the ends of the earth. Prayer does not shut me off; on the contrary, it transforms my view of the world and enables me to see life through the eyes of God. In prayer I can reach out and hold the needs of the world before the Lord. I believe that prayer has a ripple effect. My relationship with God and my response to what I believe He wants of me has an effect on others – near and far. The sacred is not found only in the extraordinary. It is in every human situation, and everything truly human finds a place in our hearts at prayer.

A man who fears suffering,
Is already suffering from what he fears

Michel de Montaigne

If you remain in me, and my words remain in you, you may ask what you will, and you shall receive it.

JOHN 15: 7

Prayer does not change God but it changes him who prays

SØREN KIERKEGAARD

You are the salt of the earth ... You are the light of the world.

MATTHEW 5: 13 & 14

They will pick up snakes in their hands, and be unharmed; and if they should drink deadly poison it shall not hurt them: they shall lay their hands upon the sick, who will recover.

MARK 16: 18

The eye with which I see God
Is the very same eye
with which God sees me

Meister Eckhart

We are called to be pioneers. Pioneers
who stand on the edge of great beginnings,
of unseen futures, Pioneers filled with
unwarranted confidence that visions give.
Pioneers whose eyes and ears are elsewhere,
who hear an echo of possibilities as music
poised to enter the universe.

PIERRE TEILHARD DE CHARDIN, SJ

The question is not what you look
at but what you see

HENRY DAVID THOREAU

*Don't judge each day by the harvest you reap
but by the seeds that you plant*

Robert Louis Stevenson

*I have come so that you may have life
and have it to the full.*

John 10: 10–11

I believe in the sun even when it is not shining
I believe in love even when I don't feel it
I believe in God
Even when he is silent

A Jewish prayer

The tragedy of life is not death
But what we let die inside of us when we live

Norman Cousins

They say God is everywhere and yet we always think of Him as somewhat of a recluse

Emily Dickinson

God enters by a private door into every individual

Ralph Waldo Emerson

What is God? He is the breath
inside the breath

KABIR

The Lord lives amongst the pots and pans

ST TERESA OF AVILA

*We're all of us children in a vast kindergarten
trying to spell God's name with the
wrong alphabet blocks*

<small>TENNESSEE WILLIAMS</small>

*My religion consists of a humble admiration of
the illimitable superior spirit who reveals himself
in the slight details we are able to perceive
with our frail and feeble minds*

<small>ALBERT EINSTEIN</small>

I am in every religion as a thread
through a string of pearls

HINDU SAYING

I hear and behold God in every object
In the faces of men and women I see God,
and in my own face in the glass;
I find letters from God dropped in the street,
and every one is signed by God's name.
And I leave them where they are, for I know
that others will punctually come for
ever and ever.

WALT WHITMAN, *LEAVES OF GRASS*

I would believe only in a God
who could dance

FRIEDRICK NIETZSCHE

If you are feeling happy, you don't have to speak
about it. Happiness is its own thing and needs
no words, it doesn't even need to be thought
about. But the instant you start to say 'I am
happy' this innocence is lost. You have created
a gap, however small, between yourself and the
genuine feeling. So do not think that when you
speak of God you are near him. Your words have
created a gap that you must cross to get back to
him. And you will never cross it with your mind.

KRISHNAMURTI

*What each one is interiorly, face to face
with God, unknown to anyone, is of vital
consequence to all; and every act of love, every
act of faith and adoration, every mute uplifting
of the heart, draws the whole world nearer
to God. From each one who is in union with
God radiates a spiritual vitality, light, strength
and joy which reaches from end to end of the
universe, a source of grace even to those least
worthy of it, even to those least conscious of it,
and knowing nothing of how or whence it come.*

ANONYMOUS

Only look and some day you will see

TONY DE MELLO

*If you remain in me and my words remain
in you, you may ask what you will and
you will receive it*

JOHN 15: 7

I am the vine,
You are the branches
Whoever remains in me and I in him,
Bears fruit in plenty,
For cut off from me
You can do nothing

John 15: 5

With candles of angels the sky is sparkled.
There's a biting frost in the wind from the hill
Bank the fire and go to bed
The soul of God will sleep in this house tonight.

Máire Mhac an tSaoi

We have become ambassadors for Christ.
It is as though God were appealing through us.

II Corinthians 5: 20

In you, O Lord, I take refuge
Let me never be put to shame
In your justice set me free
Hear me and speedily rescue me.

Be a rock of refuge for me
A mighty stronghold to save me
For you are my rock, my stronghold
For your name's sake lead me and guide me.

Release me from the snares they have hidden
For you are my refuge, Lord

Into your hands I commit my spirit
It is you who will redeem me, Lord

Psalm 31: 1–5

Ask and you shall receive;
Seek and you shall find;
Knock and it shall be opened to you.
For whoever asks, receives
Whoever seeks, finds
Whoever knocks will always have the
door opened to him

Luke 11: 9–10

If you see God within every man and woman
Then you can never do harm to any man or woman
If you see God in yourself
Then you attain perfection

Bhagavad Gita

*The greatest legacy one can pass on
to one's children and grandchildren is
not money or other material things
accumulated in one's life, but rather a
legacy of character and faith.*

BILLY GRAHAM

Celtic Christianity

Br Richard Hendrick OFM Cap.

The interplay of culture and faith has always produced unique ways of being Christian or Buddhist or Hindu or Muslim. When a faith encounters a new culture there are two possibilities – domination, which leads to resistance, fear or even violence; or fusion, which leads to a comfortable inter-being in which the best of what was is nourished by the best of what is. In the Christian tradition, this second way of being has over the centuries led to the beauty of the various Rites of the Church. Each is distinct in language, history and ritual yet all are one Church in confessing one Lord, one faith, one baptism. Unity in diversity is the very mark of the Church in its catholicity, in its universality.

In the faith communities that grew up in Europe

at its westernmost edge between the fourth and tenth centuries this accommodation to native culture, and yet illumination and completion of it by the Christian message, was undertaken in a way never seen before in the history of the Church. A faith community emerged, which though seeing itself as part of the larger Christian Church nevertheless had a unique way of being and a distinctive vision of itself, of the world and of God; a vision that is characterized today as 'Celtic'. Much of this has been lost in successive waves of invasion and ideology but the traces that remain whisper to the sacred places in many people's hearts and offer a glimpse of a way of relating to faith and to the Church that seems to ground them in this world and the next in a way both fully human and fully in communion with creation.

The 'Celtic Christians' in essence inherited an older form of Christianity from the deserts of Egypt, Lebanon, Syria and perhaps even as far away as Ethiopia. Theirs was a monastic Church, founded by monk missionaries who carried the disciplines and teachings of a contemplative form of life that completed and transformed beautifully the 'pagan' understandings of the pre-Christian Celts. Perhaps it was this origin in a monastic and contemplative way of being that led to the ready fusion of old and new, for the Christianization of the Celtic tribes and lands happened quickly, and largely without violence or persecution.

To a people who worshipped a pantheon of deities and saw the presence of the divine in every aspect of nature, the revelation of Christ and the Trinity offered a Hero and a High King as well as a God who was, at one and the same time, utterly transcendent of and gloriously immanent in his creation, so it took little to bring the pantheistic pre-Christian Celts to a more subtle understanding of a pan-en-theistic faith, especially when the transition nourished their longing and hope for an afterlife that could be gained without the sacrifice of lives in war. Awareness of the presence of the divine in and through the beauty of nature is a mark of this particular expression of Christianity: to such a degree that whilst it is present, and always has been, in the Judaeo-Christian tradition, it had never been so poetically and beautifully expressed before, and would not be again until the Franciscan School in the 1200s.

So what were these ways of being Christian that were manifested in such a unique way in the Celtic forms of Christianity?

The early Celtic Church often built on the foundations of monastic communities, each led by an elder known for their holiness and wisdom. The parallel of this structure to the tribal/clan system of the indigenous peoples under a chief meant that there was an immediate understanding, as the two systems seemed to share a common way of life despite their different origins. Loyalty to clan and to chief and through him to the High King beautifully paralleled the monks' obedience to the elder and above all to Christ, the High King of High Kings. A people raised on the sagas of the Fianna and the Red Branch Knights saw the sacrifice of one's life to an ideal, and especially to the service of a king, as noble and to be admired. Leaving home and family to serve the Gospel became attractive, even to those of royal and noble blood. This can be seen in the stories of Colm Cille (Columba) and Brigid. The so-called 'green martyrdom' of trusting in the providence of God called forth great missionaries like Brendan and Columbanus, who brought the Celtic expression of the Christian faith to parts of northern Europe and perhaps, in the case of Brendan, a good deal further. Rowing out from land into the ocean currents, they simply went wherever wind and wave, servants of the

High King of Heaven, brought them and there lived their life of prayer and praise.

Despite the lush greenness of much of the Celtic territories the spirituality of their monastics was influenced greatly by the fathers and mothers of Christian monasticism who had flourished in the deserts of Egypt and the Lebanon; large monastic complexes – often called 'Disearts' for the perceived extremity of the observance – often vied with each other in their pride in the monks and nuns who fasted the most or kept the most vigils, or whose elders worked the most miracles. This 'boasting in God' was not meant as a source of vainglory or pride: it came from the bardic culture that esteemed its heroes and heroines and commemorated their deeds to inspire the spiritual practice of others. The bardic culture of long epic poems and sagas created an educated class who, along with the druids, were among the first Christian converts; they aided in the exchange of ideas, links between cultures and cultivation of wisdom that led to the Celtic monasteries' reputation as bastions of learning and contemplative practice when the rest of Europe was falling into the chaos of the so-called Dark Ages.

In Celtic monasticism the fusion of desert

spirituality with a holistic understanding of creation and humanity's place in it saw redemption as bringing about such a healing of the person that a new and holy unity with creation was the result. Through the ancient remedies of prayer, meditation, fasting, vigils and charity, the monastic began to experience that oneness with nature that Adamic humanity first knew. We have many stories of the Celtic saints and their animal companions: Kevin and the otter, Colm Cille and his horse, Gobnait and her bees, among others, show a marvellous intimacy with our fellow creatures in which we all serve the Lord of Creation according to our capacity and gifts. The visible creation can be a door to the unseen world too. For the Celts, a liminal and animistic people, the nearness of the supernatural, the world of angels, demons and elemental powers carried over from pre-Christian days, was actively completed by the sacramental view of nature that is at the very heart of the Christian contemplative tradition in which all that exists is a word from the Word of God, and creation itself the universal testament to all peoples of all times of Divine Beauty and its nearness to us in every breath.

In the Celtic, domestic form of spirituality, every household act, no matter how small, could be performed mindfully in the presence of the divine and thus assume a cosmological and redemptive purpose and meaning. The blessing prayers and poems that come down to us from places like Donegal and Kerry and especially from the Hebrides hold an immense lexicon of benedictions for every activity and task of the day and important moments in life. The making of bread, the laying of the fire, the opening of the hall door, the kindling of the evening lights all had their blessing prayer and ritual (usually performed by women in the home and by men on the land); each had its patron saint or angel. The domestic scene, an expression of the Church in its own right, mirrored and deepened the life of the larger Church, nurturing the sense of belonging and being part of the redemptive mission of Christ through his Church.

With the turning of the year the old festivals found their fulfilment in the liturgical calendar. For example, the honouring of the ancestors at Samhain has its counterpart in the feasts of All Souls and All Saints in which the ancestors were no longer to be feared or placated but to be assisted by the prayers of the living. The old grave offerings became the blessed salt and bread left in the hearth overnight and consumed the next day. The Fires of Lughnasa became the bonfires of St John's Eve and the dancing around them continued, as did pilgrimages to holy wells and trees and mountains, places now sanctified by the observances of the saints and the miracles they wrought. 'Cuimhin an talamh na Manaigh,' the people would say ever after: 'the land remembers the monks'. So the people would gather to celebrate the goings in and goings out of life; the births, the marriages and the deaths, sanctifying them by their association with the saints of old in ruins and caves soaked in centuries of prayer.

Today, this unique spirituality and way of being Christian appeals to a generation that achingly feels its distance from the earth and her seasons, that is stressed and distressed by the pace of life and by separation from its inner rhythms. In the wave of mindfulness and meditation programmes and classes that has swept across the Western world we can detect a hunger for the wisdom of the old ways and old paths. Perhaps we need to return to the pace of the ancestors who lived with a foot in both worlds, and in domestic familiar intimacy with God; to return to a pace slow enough for us to discern the language of praise and beauty that issues from every tree and rock and rivulet of water, to realign humanity with its ancient purpose and meaning as the Celtic Christian understood it.

It would be no small thing if this wisdom was recovered and renewed for the next generation. A humble affinity with nature and a sense of our place in the cosmic context of creation and redemption would allow us to recover ourselves as pilgrims passing reverently through this world with one eye always on eternity and a heart and soul on fire for the High King of Heaven who blesses every place, every moment and every breath.

The Spirit comes to help us in our weakness, for when we cannot choose words in order to pray properly, the spirit himself expresses your plea in a way that could never be put into words.

Eternal life is here, eternal life is now

Your words are spirit, Lord
and they are life.
You have the message
of eternal life

John 6: 63 & 68

With passion pray
With passion work
With passion make love
With passion eat and drink
And dance and play
Why look like a dead fish
in this ocean of God?

Rumi

The more faithfully you listen to the voice within you, the better you will hear what is sounding outside. Only the one who listens can speak

DAG HAMMARSKJÖLD

Plunge into matter. Plunge into God. By means of all created things, without exception, the divine assails us, penetrates us and moulds us. We imagine it as distant and inaccessible, whereas in fact, we live steeped in its burning layers.

PIERRE TEILHARD DE CHARDIN, SJ

When I despair, I remember that all through history the ways of truth and love have always won. There have been tyrants, and murderers, and for a time they can seem invincible, but in the end they always fall. Think of it . . . always.

<small>MAHATMA GANDHI</small>

When you pray, you are not to be like the hypocrites; for they love to stand and pray in the synagogues and on the street corners so that they may be seen by men. Truly I say to you, they have their reward in full. But you, when you pray, go into your inner room, close your door and pray to your Father who is in secret, and your Father who sees you in secret shall repay you.

MATTHEW 6: 5–6

Street Corner Christ

I saw Christ to-day
At a street corner stand,
In the rags of a beggar he stood
He held ballads in his hand.

He was crying out: – 'Two for a penny
Will anyone buy
The finest ballads ever made
From the stuff of joy?'

But the blind and deaf went past
Knowing only there
An uncouth ballad-seller
With tail-matted hair.

And I whom men call fool
His ballads bought,
Found him whom the pieties
Have vainly sought

Patrick Kavanagh

For Peace

Health is the greatest gift
Contentment the greatest wealth
Faithfulness the best relationship

Buddha

The best thing about the future
Is that it comes one day at a time

Abraham Lincoln

If there is to be peace in the world,
There must be peace in the nations.
If there is to be peace in the nations,
There must be peace in the cities.
If there is to be peace in the cities,
There must be peace between neighbours.
If there is to be peace between neighbours,
There must be peace in the home.
If there is to be peace in the home,
There must be peace in the heart.

Lao Tzu

I hope that one day all nations great and small will be able to stand up and say we lived in pursuit of peace for all. Maybe then there will come a day when instead of saying 'God Bless America' or 'God bless some other country' everyone everywhere will say 'God bless the world'.

Martin Luther King

We are all manifestations of God
All of life, every living being and person
Is a manifestation of God
We are of God
God's spirit is walking, talking in me
Breathing through me
Not I but Christ
The prince of peace
May I be peace in the world

Sr Stan

Contemplative Prayer

Sr Aneta, Redemptoristin

Then Jacob awoke from his sleep and said,
'Surely the LORD is in this place; and I did not know it.'

Gen. 28: 16–17

'I look at Him, and He looks at me'

Contemplative prayer reminds me of a story I heard
or read years ago, taken from the life of St John Maria
Vianney, the holy priest from the French village of
Ars. One day he came to the church and saw a man
who spent a lot of time there. When the priest asked
him what he was doing, he simply answered: 'I look at
Him, and He looks at me.'

That's it! Simple as that. These words could also
be used for the experience of adoration of the Most
Blessed Sacrament.

Looking at God is important for Redemptoristine sisters, and Maria Celeste Crostarosa, our Mother, often speaks of it in her writings: He says, 'Look always at Me, in purity, in everything, even in the smallest thing.'

Is it really enough to define contemplation? Even though the practice of contemplative prayer can be quite demanding, the prayer itself is one of simplicity. God is not complicated! And his gift of contemplative prayer is as universal as the call to holiness.

Through Him, and in Him and with Him

I grew up in a Catholic family of regular churchgoers. However, it didn't make a true believer of me. This changed when I started my studies and met other young people, who wanted to live a real Christian life. Inspired by our student pastor, I too received a kind of inner light, allowing me a much better understanding of what it means to say: 'I believe in God. He has the first place in my life. My relationship with Him is not just a part of my life: it is EVERYTHING!' This insight changed a lot for me. Prayer is the most intimate encounter with the most important person in my life! It is the finest and deepest expression that Jesus Christ is the Lord of my life. I surrender everything to Him.

The deepest reality of Christian life is that we were made for God, and in our capacity to know and to love what is highest we can be raised up to participate in true union in the fullness of the life of God. René Voillaume in *The Need for Contemplation* writes:

All the great Christian contemplatives are at one in their witness. Whatever their spiritual road, union with God is seen as real – as having a reality more deeply imbedded in experience, more surely established, more firmly rooted in being and certainty, than any experience known in the material world. In this sense, it is true to say that the contemplatives are, of all people, the most realistic.

He is faithful, and He promised to come to us, with the Father and the Holy Spirit, and make His dwelling in us. We only have to love Him! Voillaume also writes:

Christians, you have chosen to give your life to Love: to the love of God, once and for all, unconditionally. The Lord has

called you, as He has called the bride in the Song of Songs.
Not that it would be right to become lost in dreams and
illusions . . . We should, nevertheless, believe to the point
of surrendering our entire life to a Love that is unlike any
other. If Christianity has a witness to give to the world, it is
to show that, in choosing to follow Christ, we have chosen
to surrender ourselves to this Love, and that this same Love
so stamps our behaviour that people of good will can have
at least an inkling that it is this which actuates our lives.

I come in silence into His presence and I let God be
God in me, speaking to me, working in me . . . Loving
me. I look at Him, listen to Him, with my heart. It is
a process that transforms me and leads me to a union
with God. I enter into the Mystery of God in me.

St John of the Cross tells us that 'To contemplate
is to receive'. Contemplative prayer is a gift. And in
Prayer and Contemplation Mark Gibbard explains that
'Contemplation for me is perceiving receptively . . .
Through this receiving love and responding with love
we grow more and more into those real, mature men
and women God wishes us to be – those men and
women he desires to use in the transformation of the
world.'

Battlefields and dark nights

Receiving is simple, yet so difficult for us because we are not good receivers! It sounds paradoxical, as we normally like to receive gifts. But the gift of God seems to embarrass us. We have to stand before him with empty hands, and emptying ourselves can be very demanding. Surrendering everything to him, every single part of our being, every experience, thought, emotion, plans, opinion, desire . . . No imagination, no expectations, no words . . .

Henri Nouwen writes in *Clowning in Rome*, 'Prayer is a radical conversion of all our mental processes, because in prayer we move away from ourselves – our worries, preoccupations, and self-gratifications – and direct all that we recognize as ours to God in the simple trust that through His love all will be made new.' This is far from easy! Nouwen continues:

> There is a deep resistance to making ourselves so vulnerable, so naked, so totally unprotected. We indeed want to love God and worship Him, but we also want to keep a little corner of our inner life for ourselves, where we can hide and think our own secret thoughts, dream our dreams, and play with our own mental fabrications.

And that can lead us to idolatry: 'We limit His lordship and erect little altars to the mental images we do not want to submit to a divine conversation.'

Choosing the path of contemplation implies choosing this constant struggle and purification. St Teresa of Avila speaks about it in her *Interior Castle*: you have to fight against sin, but she asks that we keep our eyes fixed not on the enemies, but on Jesus Christ, putting our desires into God's hands and remembering that everything is possible in Him. We learn to see ourselves as we really are, and discover our sinfulness in a way that we never have before. Sin is ugly – so this experience is not pleasant. Many feel discouraged and turn back. Yes, it is dark, but still: it is the night of love! If we continue on this way, we will grow and make a place for Christ in our lives.

Richard Rohr also speaks of letting go every false image or idea we have about ourselves. We must just stand before God in all our nakedness. But there is good news: 'When we are nothing, we are in a fine position to receive everything from God.' Or, in the words of Mother Teresa of Calcutta, 'God cannot fill what is already full'!

Richard Rohr writes: 'The contemplative stance is the Third Way. We stand in the middle . . . neither fighting nor fleeing, we are in the place of grace out of which newness comes. Creativity comes from here, and we can finally do a new thing for the world. We can stop building our kingdom and become usable in the kingdom of God.'

Fruits and ministry

Contemplation changes our perception of reality, and enables us to recognize and respond to God's presence in everything. Henri Nouwen writes: 'The contemplative is someone who sees the things for what they really are, who sees the real connections, who knows – as Thomas Merton used to say – "what the scoop" is'.

Contemplative prayer brings healing into our relationships: with God, with others and with ourselves. Nouwen also speaks about relationships with nature and with time:

It is the movement from nature as a property to be possessed to nature as gift to be received with admiration and gratitude. It is the movement from time as [a] randomly thrown-together series of incidents and accidents to time as a constant opportunity for a change of heart.

In our Redemptorist spirituality, 'The constant contemplation of the mysteries of Christ will develop in us this mark of happy and radiant joy, of simplicity and true charity which we consider a characteristic of our community' (*Const.* 10).

Daily contemplation makes a transforming celebration of the daily Eucharist. As Nouwen explains: 'The Eucharist became again the place from which and to which I might live; and it made me realize that even the most private form of contemplation is, in the final analysis, a service to the whole community.'

Whether I am active or whether I am praying, whether
I laboriously open my soul through work, or whether
God assails my soul with passivities of growth or of
diminishment – I am equally conscious in all instances to
be united to Christ … First, foremost and always I am in
Christ Jesus. And only then do I act, or do I suffer,
or do I contemplate. (Teilhard de Chardin)

Hail Mary . . .

Mother Teresa, when asked why she did what she did, answered: 'I do it for Jesus.' And then she added,

'Through Mary.' Mary, Holy Virgin and Mother of God, is the best teacher of contemplative prayer – through the gift of the Rosary prayer.

'The most important reason for strongly encouraging the practice of the Rosary is that it represents a most effective means of fostering among the faithful that *commitment to the contemplation of the Christian mystery* . . . The Rosary belongs among the finest and most praiseworthy traditions of Christian contemplation,' John Paul II wrote, in his Apostolic Letter, *Rosarium Virginis Mariae*, of 2002. And according to Constitution 8 of the Congregation of the Most Holy Redeemer, 'We love to contemplate the marvels worked by the Lord in Mary and we strive to achieve an even truer and deeper Marian devotion.'

Nothing could be simpler.

Bibliography

St Teresa of Avila, *Interior Castle*, Forgotten Books edition, 2007.

Constitutions and Statutes, Order of the Most Holy Redeemer, General Curia C.Ss.R., Rome, 2002.

Mark Gibbard, *Prayer and Contemplation*, Mowbray, London, 1976.

Thomas Merton, *Contemplative Prayer*, Darton, Longman & Todd, London, 2005.

Francis Kelly Nemeck, OMI and Marie Theresa Coombs, Hermit, *Contemplation,* Wipf & Stock Publishers, Eugene, Oregon, 2001.

Henri J. M. Nouwen, *Clowning in Rome. Reflections on Solitude, Celibacy, Prayer, and Contemplation*, Image, Colorado Springs, CO, 2000.

Richard Rohr, *Everything Belongs: The gift of contemplative prayer,* Crossroads Publishing Co., 2003.

René Voillaume, *The Need for Contemplation*, Darton, Longman & Todd, London, 1972.

Every visible or invisible creature is a theophany or appearance of God.

St John Scotus Eriugena (Eoin Erinnacht)

And if tonight my soul may find her peace
in sleep, and sink in good oblivion,
and in the morning wake like a new-opened flower
then I have been dipped again in God, and new-created

D. H. Lawrence, 'Shadows'

*Never be in a hurry; do everything quietly
and in a calm spirit. Do not lose your inner
peace for anything whatsoever, even if
your whole world seems upset.*

ST FRANCIS DE SALES

May there be peace in the higher regions;
may there be peace in the firmament;
may there be peace on earth.
May the waters flow peacefully;
may the herbs and plants grow peacefully;
may all the divine powers bring unto us peace.
The supreme Lord is peace.
May we all be in peace, peace, and only peace;
and may that peace come unto each of us.
Shanti Shanti Shanti!

The Vedas

To laugh often and much
To win the respect of intelligent people and the
affection of children;
To earn the approbation of honest critics and endure
the betrayal of false friends:
To appreciate beauty, to find the best in others;
to give of oneself;
To leave the world a bit better, whether by a healthy
child, a garden patch, or a redeemed social condition;
to have played and laughed with enthusiasm and sung
with exultation;
To know even one life has breathed easier because
you have lived:
This is to have succeeded

Ralph Waldo Emerson

*The fruit of all study is to perceive the eternal
word of God reflected in every
plant and insect, every bird and animal,
and every man and woman.*

ST NINIAN

For Blessings

May God let his face shine on you
And be gracious to you
May God show his face to you
and bring you peace

Numbers 6: 26

Deep peace of the running wave to you.
Deep peace of the flowing air to you.
Deep peace of the quiet earth to you.
Deep peace of the shining stars to you.
Deep peace of the gentle night to you.

Celtic benediction

Do all the good you can
By all the means you can
In all the ways you can
In all the places you can
To all the people you can
As long as ever you can

John Wesley, quoted in A Grateful Heart

May the road rise up to meet you.
May the wind be always at your back.
May the sun shine warm upon your face;
the rains fall soft upon your fields and until we meet again,
may God hold you in the palm of His hand

Irish blessing

May your life be like a wild flower
Growing freely in the beauty
And joy of each day

Native American proverb

To Pray is to Love

Jean Vanier

I'd love to be able to pray. I have a desire to be with Jesus and to walk with him.

Sometimes I am in a bit of a fog or feel lost. But I am told that a desire to pray is already a prayer. Then there are the times when I can rest in Jesus. Yes, prayer is rest.

And there are all those moments in the day when I am taken up and too busy – things to do, people to see … The telephone rings. The motor inside me starts up too quickly. Away it goes, maybe fuelled by anguish.

How to re-find myself at such moments? The Book of Revelations (the Apocalypse) reveals the Lord knocking at the door of my heart. If I hear him and stop the motor, if I let him enter into my heart we can eat together. Jesus becomes my friend. I can become his beloved brother.

Sometimes Jesus knocks at the door of my heart through a person crying out in need. If I hear that person, let her in, and eat with her, we can become friends. It becomes a friendship with Jesus and in Jesus.

To pray is to love, to offer myself in the sunshine or in the night. It is always good to be with Jesus. John in his letter says that 'love is of God and the person who loves is born of God and knows God'. So the important thing is to love, to die to our egoism and rise up in friendship with Jesus.

Hold on to what is good
even if it is
a handful of earth.

Hold on to what you believe
even if it is a tree which stands by itself.

Hold on to what you must do
even if it is a long way from here.

Hold on to life
even if it is easier letting go.

Hold on to my hand
even if I have gone away from you.

Pueblo Indian blessing

Sense the blessings of the earth in the perfect arc of a ripe tangerine, the taste of warm, fresh bread, the circling flight of birds, the lavender colour of the sky shining in a late-afternoon rain puddle, the million times we pass other beings in our cars and shops and out among the trees without crashing, conflict, or harm.

JACK KORNFIELD

May you have warm words on a cold evening
A full moon on a dark night
and the road downhill
all the way to your door
And may you be in heaven three
days before the devil know you're dead

An Irish wish

May there always be work for your hands to do.
May your purse always hold a coin or two.
May the sun always shine on your windowpane.
May a rainbow be certain to follow each rain.
May the hand of a friend always be near you.
May God fill your heart with gladness to cheer you.

An Irish blessing

May each of us inspire good actions always

Buddha

And the wind said
May you be as strong as the oak,
yet flexible as the birch
may you stand as tall as the redwood,
live gracefully as the willow
and may you always bear fruit
all your days on this earth

Native American prayer

Out of his infinite glory, may he give you the power through his Spirit for your hidden self to grow strong, so that Christ may live in your hearts through faith, and then, planted in love and built on love, you will with all the saints have strength to grasp the breadth and the length, the height and the depth; until, knowing the love of Christ, which is beyond all knowledge, you are filled with the utter fullness of God

EPHESIANS 3: 16–19

May he support us all day long
Till the shades lengthen and evening comes
And the busy world is hushed
And the fever of life is over
And our work is done
Then in his mercy
May he give us a safe lodging
And a holy rest
And peace at the last

Cardinal Newman

And when your eyes freeze behind the grey window
And the ghost of loss gets in to you,
May a flock of colours,
Indigo, red, green and azure blue,
Come to awaken in you
A meadow of delight . . .
And so may a slow wind
work these words of love around you,
an invisible cloak to mind your life

John O'Donohue, 'Beannacht' ('Blessing')

May the Lord bless you
May the Lord protect and guide you
May his strength uphold you
His peace surround you
His love enfold you
May the Lord bless and keep you

Old Irish saying

And every evening at sun-down
I ask a blessing on the town,
For whether we last the night or no
I'm sure is always touch-and-go

Dylan Thomas, The Rev. Jenkins' evening prayer,
Under Milk Wood

May the Power of God this day enable me
The nakedness of God disarm me
The beauty of God silence me
The justice of God give me voice
The integrity of God hold me
The desire of God move me
The fear of God expose me to the truth
The breath of God give me abundant life

Janet Morley

Deep peace of the rolling waves to you
Deep peace of the flowing air to you
Deep peace of the quiet earth to you
Deep peace of the shining stars to you
Deep peace of the Son of Peace to you
Amen

Gaelic blessing

Instructions for Meditation:

Fr Seraphion of Mount Athos

When you meditate, be like a mountain
Immovably set in silence.
Its thoughts are rooted in eternity.
Do not do anything, just sit, be
And you will reap the fruit flowing from your prayer.

When you meditate, be like a flower
Always directed towards the sun.
Its stalk, like a spine, is always straight.
Be open, ready to accept everything without fear
And you will not lack light on your way.

When you meditate, be like an ocean
Always immovable in its depth.
Its waves come and go.
Be calm in your heart
And evil thoughts will go away by themselves.

(Continued)

When you mediate, remember your breath:
Thanks to it we have come alive.
It comes from God and returns to God
Unite the word of prayer with the stream of life
(the breath),
And nothing will separate you from the Giver of life.

When you meditate, be like a bird
Singing without a rest in front of the Creator.
Its song rises like the smoke of incense.
Let your prayer be like the coo of a dove,
And you will never succumb to discouragement.

When you meditate, be like Abraham
Giving his son as an offering.
It was a sign that he was ready to sacrifice everything.
You too, leave everything,
And in your loneliness God will be with you.

When you meditate it is Jesus
Praying in you to the Father in the Spirit.
You are carried by the flame of his love.
Be like a river, serving all,
And the time will come, when you will change into Love.

Every mountain teaches us the sense of eternity,
Every flower, when it fades, teaches us the sense of
fleetingness.
The ocean teaches us, how to retain peace during
adversities,
And love always teaches us to love.

Contributors' Biographies

Sr Marie Fahy is a Cistercian nun in St Mary's Abbey, Glencairn, Lismore, Co. Waterford. She has been serving as Abbess since 2001.

St Mary's Abbey is the only Cistercian monastery for women in Ireland. In 2014 the Abbey appeared in the 'Would You Believe?' documentary *School Of Love*, which can be found on their website. Many people join them in the praying of the daily Office and come to stay at the guest house for private retreats, silence and contemplation, and to align themselves with the contemplative rhythm there (http://www.glencairnabbey.org/).

BR RICHARD HENDRICK is a priest-friar of the Irish province of the Capuchin Franciscan order. For the past twenty years he has worked to bring the riches of the Christian contemplative tradition to young people at both second and third levels. He is one of the founders of the 'Sanctuary for Schools' programmes developed at the Sanctuary centre, Stanhope Street, Dublin, which seeks to offer the wisdom of the different world meditative traditions as an answer to the challenges many young people face on the path to adulthood today.

ANNE MARIE MAGUIRE is the author of *Hidden Contemplatives*, and a lay Associate of St Mary's Abbey, Glencairn. She is a naturopath and herbalist and has taught T'ai Chi and Meditation. She has worked for German, Australian and Irish companies, writing spiritual and corporate material. Based in the countryside of Cork, she currently writes on contemplation and interior spirituality (http://www.hiddencontemplatives.ie/).

SR MARY MAGDALEN grew up in Clonakilty, Co. Cork, known as Maura Dineen. Her parents founded a secondary school for boys there because secondary education for poor boys was not otherwise available at that time. Her mother and father's strong faith and their total dedication to the task entrusted to them by God had a profound influence on her as she grew up. Having completed her Leaving Certificate in the local Convent of Mercy, Maura went on to University College, Cork, graduating with a Pass Arts degree in English, History and French. She also studied Introductory Philosophy in her First Year. After a brief period of teaching in Scotland, she finally answered God's call to consecrate her life completely to God in Carmelite Order, in Loughrea, Co. Galway, in 1972 where she still lives today.

Sr Bernardine Meskell was born in a little village, Castleconnell, outside Limerick, the eldest of eight children. She went to boarding school in Spanish Point, Co. Clare, and entered the Poor Clare Monastery, Ennis, in 1963 where she has spent fifty-two very happy years with a beautiful community of Poor Clare sisters.

Sr Regina McHugh was born in Raharney, Mullingar, Co. Westmeath. After secondary school in Loreto, Mullingar, she trained as a nurse in Jervis Street

Hospital, Dublin. Regina spent some time nursing in Bangladesh and as a public health nurse on the Aran Islands, after which she entered the Poor Clare community in Ennis. Sr Regina has lived happily in this community for thirty-one years.

SR ANETA was born in a small town in the south-west of Poland in 1971. Just before she started her university studies in Wroclaw, she experienced God's loving Presence in her life in a very deep way. In early 1993 she entered the Monastery of Redemptoristine Nuns in Brugge, Belgium. After twenty years in Flanders, she joined the community in Drumcondra in Dublin.

JOHN O'DONOHUE wrote several international bestselling books, including *Anam Cara*, *Eternal Echoes*, *Divine Beauty*, *Benedictus* and *The Four Elements*. John also published *Person als Vermittlung* on the philosophy of Hegel and two collections of poetry, *Echoes of Memory* and *Conamara Blues*. He lectured across Europe and the USA and lived in Conamara.

JEAN VANIER, Ph.D. (L'Institut Catholique de Paris), is the founder of L'Arche, an international network of communities where people with and without intellectual disabilities experience life together as fellow human beings who share a mutuality of care and need. His books include *Community and Growth*, *Becoming Human*, *From Brokenness to Community* and *Befriending the Stranger*.

The essay entitled 'Growing in Prayer', was written by a member of the Order of the Poor Clare Sisters in Dublin.